# How Norwich Fought Against the Plague

*Rood screen panel at St. Mary's Church, Sparham, c. 1480. The Latin inscription reads, 'I should have been as though I had not been born, I should have been carried from the womb to the grave'.*

# How Norwich Fought Against the Plague

## Lessons from the Past

Frank Meeres

POPPYLAND
PUBLISHING

This edition 2021 published by Poppyland Publishing, Lowestoft, NR32 3BB.

www.poppyland.co.uk

ISBN 978 1 909796 82 9

Designed and typeset in 10.5 on 13.5 pt Gilgamesh Pro.

Printed by Ashford Colour Press.

Picture credits:

Author's collection, 6, 11, 12, 14, 17, 25, 32, 33 (bottom), 36, 43, 57, 64, 73, 80, 94, 95, 101, 130
Norfolk Record Office, 18, 28, 30, 33 (top), 45, 55, 56, 70, 79, 96, 99
Poppyland Ltd. collection, front cover, title page (opposite), 26
Wikimedia, 1 (opposite) under Creative Commons licence
Map B drawn by John Fone for his 'Index to Norwich Marriages 1813-1837' (1982)

Royalties on this book have been kindly donated by the author to the Norfolk Archives and Heritage Development Foundation, partner charity of the Norfolk Record Office.

Front cover, part of a rood screen St. Mary's church, Sparham.

# Contents

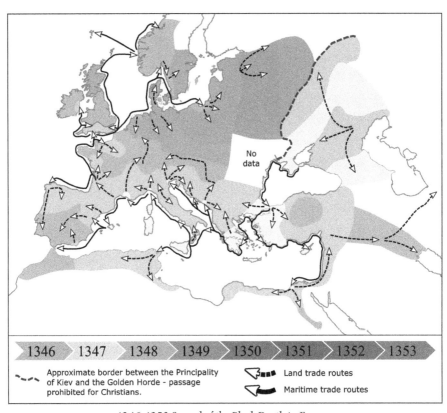

| 1346 | 1347 | 1348 | 1349 | 1350 | 1351 | 1352 | 1353 |

No
data

- - - Approximate border between the Principality
of Kiev and the Golden Horde - passage
prohibited for Christians.

Land trade routes

Maritime trade routes

*1346-1353 Spread of the Black Death in Europe.*

# Introduction

THE plague was in England for three hundred years, first arriving in a wave of mortality known as the Black Death in 1348-9, then in a series of attacks at different dates in different places, until the final outbreaks of 1665-6. There are no direct records of deaths in 1348-9, but the cumulative evidence is that 40-50% of the population died in that summer alone. More localised attacks over later years could kill a third or more of the population in a particular town, with all the effects that such a drop in the number of people would cause.

People did not know how the plague spread and therefore how to prevent it. In the Middle Ages, it was thought that the plague was a direct punishment by God for sin, and it was often compared to the Great Flood in the days of Noah. The only defence therefore was to lead an improved moral life, in the hope that this would be more pleasing to God. In later centuries, as the plague re-occurred, cities did take measures to try to prevent the spread, and we shall see what steps the Norwich authorities took at different times.

How did people actually catch plague? We now know that the plague was carried in the fleas of rats and could spread from rats to people. A flea with the disease could live away from a rat for several months, for example in a bundle of cloth, so you might never see a rat but could still be bitten by a flea. When the plague entered the human body through the bite of a flea, it would be carried through the body to the nearest lymph node where it would multiply by millions, causing a swelling. Most flea bites were on the legs, so these swellings were usually in the groin, but they could be under the armpits or behind the ear. This process took between three and eight days. After another three or four days, the plague would reach the blood stream and carry the infection to the organs, especially the spleen and the lungs, resulting - usually - in death.

It was also possible to catch the plague directly from someone who already had it, by breathing it in from the moisture of a cough, or by breathing it in from bedding infected with the faeces of a flea. This was a much quicker death, as the plague would go straight into the lungs - death would follow within two days. The sudden death caused by catching the plague from a sneeze is often said to have given rise to the child's nursery rhyme:

Ring a ring of roses,
A pocket full of posies,

1

A-tishoo, A-tishoo:
ALL FALL DOWN!

However, this is not the case: plague did not make people sneeze, and the song is much later in origin. Folklore expert Steve Roud comments:

The plague origin is complete nonsense, and was almost certainly invented, probably in the 1940s or 1950s, by someone extrapolating from the word 'posy' in the rhyme and then bending all other 'evidence' to fit.[1]

Some authorities think there was a third form of plague where, when it was in the human blood stream, it could be taken into a human flea, and spread by it when it bit another human being. This may have occurred but does not seem to have been common.

Now the science. The plague is caused by a rod-shaped bacterium, YERSINIA PESTIS: it was not identified until 1894, and is named after its discoverer, Alexandre Yersin. It is still found today in many parts of the world, but not in Europe. In the USA, for example, there are an average of 10-15 infections a year. Most victims are under the age of 20, with males and females equally at risk. It is also found in countries in Asia, Africa and South America.

Yersinia pestis causes three types of illness:

Bubonic Plague, the most common type: an incubation period of two to eight days (but occasionally as long as a month) led to high temperature, headache, vomiting, exhaustion and abdominal pain. Swollen lymph glands ('buboes') developed in the groin, armpits or neck. Bleeding under the skin produced the black gangrenous patches known as 'tokens': these were the main signs by which Searchers defined a dead body as being a victim of plague. Plague killed about half of those who caught it, a rate far higher than that of Covid in 2020.

Pneumonic plague, affecting the lungs, leading to the spitting out of blood. This form can be spread from person to person by coughs and sneezes, or even breathing.

Septicaemic plague—where there is blood infection: the bacteria enter the blood stream. This type was the least common, but also the most deadly.

The bacterium's 'reservoir species', in which it is endemic and largely non-lethal, are rodents and other small mammals. Transmission to humans is often through the bite of rat fleas: the fleas can live for months away from rats in an object like a bundle of wool, so can be spread even when there are no rats present. Exposure to dead rodents or rabbits is also a factor. Pneumonic plague is spread directly from human being to human being by droplet infection.

## Spread

The plague has always existed in Central Asia and China. In the 1330s it suddenly began to spread outwards, perhaps because of very exceptional weather conditions: Hubert Lamb calls the rains and flooding in the area 'one of the greatest weather disasters ever known'.[2]

The plague was in southern Russia by 1345-6, reached Constantinople in 1347 and Italy later in the same year: it travelled on rats which were on the ships trading across the Mediterranean. There are several European witnesses that describe the plague, for example:

Contemporary Italian writer **Giovanni Boccaccio** noted:

> it showed itself in a sad and wonderful manner. Here (Florence) there appeared tumours under the armpits and on the groin some as big as apples, others the size of an egg. Afterwards purple spots in most parts of the body, some large and few in number, others smaller and more numerous - both kinds the harbingers of death.

The fourteenth century Italian historian **Giovanni Villani** wrote:

> it took men generally in the head or stomach appearing first in the groin or under the armpits by knots or swellings called boils, blains or plague sores, attended with devouring fever with spitting or vomiting blood, whence for the most part they died presently or within a day or two at most.

**Guido de Chauliac**, the great surgeon who nobly stayed in Avignon for six months when the visitation was the worst, also mentions the carbuncular swellings in the groin and axillae, the purple spots, the violent inflammation of the lungs attended by the fearful expectoration of blood.

The spread of the Black Death seemed rapid to contemporaries, but to those who have experienced how rapidly infection can travel in an age of air travel, its progress seems slow but inexorable. It reached Avignon in southern France in the spring of 1348 and was in Paris by June. It crossed over to England in the early summer of 1348, probably from a ship landing at a West Country port. Several chronicles, including that of the Grey Friars in Lynn, say Melcombe Regis (adjoining Weymouth), often fixing the date as being around the date of the feast of St John the Baptist (24 June). However, the Black Death was certainly present in Devon before that: on 16 June, no sheriff's man could appear before the exchequer as they had all died of plague![3] Other chroniclers cite Bristol or Southampton as the point of first entry, and it could of course have arrived on several different ships at more or less the same time. It certainly seems to have first appeared in the West Country: then, spreading slowly (by modern standards) but inevitably across the country, by autumn it had reached London.

The plague could be seen to be spreading across the country, but no one knew the cause: various bishops issued warning letters, urging a return to a supposed higher standard of morality that had existed in the past. One of the first was a letter from the Archbishop of York, written as early as 28 July 1348: 'there can be no one who does not know, since it is now public knowledge, how great a mortality, pestilence and infection of the air are now threatening various parts of the world, and especially England ... the only hope is to hurry back to Him alone whose mercy outweighs justice'. On 24 October 1348, the Bishop of Winchester wrote to all the clergy in his diocese about 'this most savage pestilence, more cruel than a two-edged sword.' He recommended contrition, confession of sins and the performance of penances—and processions of the clergy and prayers.[4]

In January 1349, the Bishop of Bath and Wells went further. He pointed out how vital it was for a dying person to confess his sins before death: at such a time of crisis it might be impossible to find a priest to hear your confession, so it might be necessary to confess to a layman—and even, as a last resort and if no man could be found, to a *woman*! The fifteenth century world had indeed turned upside down.

## Notes

1    Steve Roud, *The Lore of the Playground* (2010) p.283.

2    H H Lamb, *Climate, History and the Modern World* (1995 edition) p.200.

3    Harold Fox, 'Peasant farmers. patterns of settlement and pays' in Robert Higham (ed) *Landscape and Townscape in the South West* (1989).

4    Rosemary Horrox, editor, *The Black Death* (1994) pp.111, 175.

# The Black Death in Norwich, 1349

WE do not know how many people were living in Norwich before the plague struck in 1349. Estimates are really little more than guesses. Jim Bolton writes:

> At Norwich, England's second or third city, with a pre-plague population of some 10-12,000, the plague arrived in January 1349 and raged until spring 1350. Perhaps 40-45% of the population died.' P Lindley makes a higher guess: 'East Anglia, indeed, seems to have been particularly hard hit by the plague. Norwich, with a population of well over 13,000 before the plague, lost over half its citizens and not only did it never recover its position in relation to the rest of England but, in absolute terms, had barely regained its vanished population by the end of the sixteenth century.[1]

More recent work has suggested that the population of Norwich was considerably higher than previously thought. Elizabeth Rutledge has looked at tithing records for the two parishes of St Peter Mancroft and St Stephen and extrapolated from these that the population was between 15,000 and 17,000 in 1311, 'rising to nearly 25,000 by 1333'.[2]

Philip Ziegler says that the plague reached East Anglia in March, peaking in the summer months of May to July. The manor court rolls for Hunstanton confirm this chronology: they show no effects of the plague in March, but many deaths in April and these deaths continue throughout the summer months, stopping only in October. The chronicle of the Lynn Grey Friars' says the same, 'In 1349 at about Easter or a little earlier, pestilence broke out in East Anglia and lasted for the whole summer'.[3]

A crisis like that of the Black Death would today produce an enormous amount of documentary material. Things were very different in 1349: few records were made, and not all of these have survived. One key difference is in the recording of individual lives. Since 1837, every birth and death in the country has been recorded. Between 1538 and 1837, although there was not a registration system of births and deaths, each church kept a record of baptisms and burials. Before 1538, there was no kind of registration at all: names are only recorded when

*Representation of Norwich at the time of the Black Death.*

one person succeeds to the property or official job of another. We can look at some examples of the forms of record for 1349 that tell us about these groups of people: even where there are obviously an unusual number of deaths, the plague will almost never be directly mentioned as the cause of the upheaval.

The three principal types of sources are the archives of the city of Norwich; the records of the Church; and, for the areas outside Norwich, manor records.

## 1. THE CITY ARCHIVES

The great eighteenth century historian, Francis Blomefield, looked at the city archives and found this evidence in the **Norwich Mayor's Book**:

> In 1348, Jan 1, the plague broke out in this city, from which time, to the first of July following, as our historians assure us, there died no less than 57,104 (or more rightly as others have it, 57,374) persons, in this city only, besides religious and beggars; the great numbers that all historians agreed died here in this mortality, surprise some, who imagine, that because there are not so many now in the whole city there must be a mistake in the figures, but there is not, for thus sith the best record for this purpose, 'In this yere was swiche a dethe in Norwic that there died of ye pestilence 57,374 beside religious and beggars', and our historian afore quoted is only mistaken as to the time, it being computed from Jan 1 1348 to Jan 1 1349, namely a whole year.

Blomefield made his own deductions from what he saw as the recorded facts. He guessed that there might have been over a thousand people in each parish in the city and that there were over 70 places of divine worship, so that the population of Norwich before 1349, including its suburbs, could have been over 70,000. Stow gives a similar figure. He says that between 1 January and 1 July in Norwich, 57,104 people died of plague: he excludes 'ecclesiastical mendicants and Dominicans' (meaning, friars).

Blomefield also quotes a passage from the **Norwich 'Book of Pleas'**:

In the year of Our Lord 1349, God Almighty visited mankind with a deadly plague which began in the south parts of the world, and went through even the north parts thereof, attacking all nations of the world: this plague equally destroyed Christians, Jews and Saracens, killed the confessor and the confesses in many places this plague did not leave the fifth part of the people alive, it struck the world with great fear, so great was the pestilence, that the like was never seen, heard, nor read of before, for it was believed, that there was not a greater number of souls destroyed by the flood in the days of Noah, than died by this plague.

Blomefield is quoting from two different volumes among the Norwich city archives. That from the Book of Pleas is a dramatic quotation, but it is not meant to describe Norwich in particular, but rather to describe the whole world. It is actually a copy of a chronicle written in Louth Abbey in Lincolnshire and copied word by word into the Norwich book.

The actual figure comes from a list of events in the Mayor's Book. This book was not even bought by the city until 1526 so it is in no sense contemporary evidence.

Other evidence comes from the lists of names of the bailiffs of the city. There were four of these, appointed for a year: but they could serve the office on more than one occasion. Do these names suggest a great change happening at the end of the 1340s? I have looked at the lists: in the 1330s, 29 men served as bailiff, five serving twice and three serving three times. In the 1340s, 33 men served as bailiff, seven serving twice. Fourteen of the men had served in the previous decade. In the 1350s, 35 men served, three serving twice and one serving three times. They included fourteen men who had served in the 1340s, so there had been **no** sudden mortality amongst these group of men. Historians, William Hudson and J C Tingey, confirm my figures: according to their calculations, of 54 men named in the ten years before 1350, 27 are known 'from various sources' to have survived.[4]

## Title Deeds

Norwich has a series of enrolled deeds recording, among other things, transfers of property in the city. Unfortunately, there is a gap of 37 years in the series, from 1340 to 1377. Fifteen of the title deeds from which the rolls would have been subscribed do survive for the year 1349, and a further three deeds for the same year survive among the archives of Norwich Cathedral. Of the fifteen deeds, two are wills and are discussed below. The most important of the others is a grant of 16 September 1349 by the bailiffs of the city: they grant to Robert Bendiste, citizen, a *vacant* place in the parish of St Peter Mancroft, for which he agrees to pay rent. Here is direct evidence that, presumably because of the death of its former owner and any heirs he may have had, that here is unclaimed property in the centre of the city.

Several of the other deeds suggest there has been a recent death. Another property in St Peter Mancroft, in this case described as a shop, was sold by Adam de Illington in September 1349: he had bought it from the executors of Thomas Pestissane. In the same month, the executor of the late Robert Papungey, saddler, disposes of his property in St Mary the Less to his widow. In November 1349, John le Cook sells tenements and rents that he had bought from Matilda, the daughter of Geoffrey de Earlham: she is still alive as she quitclaims the new owner of any claim she has, but her father may have recently died and can have left no male heir as his daughter has inherited.

Two deeds relating to the property of the Godyng family in St Matthew suggest possible family deaths in 1349. In July, a brew house belonging formerly to Richard Godyng is sold off by William Godyng, presumably his relative. In December, William's daughter is involved in the sale of the property formerly owned by her father. Perhaps Richard and William Godyng have died in quick succession. We know from other evidence (see below) that there was a high mortality rate in the parish of St Matthew, which was on Holme Street, near the Great Hospital.

## Freemen of Norwich

Penny Dunn says: 'The largest number of entrants for any year in the history to the **Liber Introitus Civicum** or Old Free Book, is recorded in 1349-50, when 120 men paid to join the Norwich franchise. In the previous year only twenty-one individuals had taken up the privilege and it seems that immigrants from outside Norwich were mostly responsible for the gradual provision of new citizens in the months following the loss of so many leading residents'.[5]

Seventeen new freemen were registered on the Translation of St Edward 1349 (13 October 1349), and 70 on the Saturday after the Feast of the

Circumcision 1350 (3 January 1350). In terms of occupations, 24 of these 87 men have occupational surnames including three skinners, two mercers, two cutlers, two baxters (bakers) and two clerks, and the others having a wide variety of occupation. In terms of location, about 60 have names indicating the place from which they come, and these embrace a large number of Norfolk villages, especially along the Yare valley, the areas around Wroxham, Dereham and Swaffham. Some are very local such as 'John de Bracondale, mercer', while only two have names definitely suggesting that they have come from outside Norfolk: Semannus of Beccles, in Suffolk but only 20 miles from Norwich, and Thomas of Leighton Buzzard, in Bedfordshire and about 110 miles from Norwich. I have listed the names of these incomers, beneficiaries of the high mortality caused by the Black Death in the city, in Appendix One. There is one man from further afield among the 28 new freemen in the following year: Simon de Almannia, but most of the losses among city trades appear to have been made up by recruiting from within the county.

## The City Assembly Records

Two actions taken by the City in the twenty years after the Black Death, show that there had been a crisis and that it was still ongoing:

1.  Assembly of 19 November 1354 (from the Book of Customs)

    Whereas great injuries and dangers so often have happened before this time in the City of Norwich and still happen from day to day in so much as boars, sows and pigs before this time and still go vagrant by day and night without a keeper in the said city, whereby divers persons and children have thus been hurt by boars, children killed and eaten and others buried exhumed, and others maimed, and many persons of the said city have received great injuries as wrecking of houses, destruction of gardens of divers persons by such kind of pigs upon which great complaint is often brought before the said bailiffs and community imploring them for remedy on the misfortunes, dangers and injuries which have been done to them.

    The Assembly ordered that pigs were to be kept in their enclosures: any pig found going at large without a keeper could freely be killed. Every pig owner could let their pig out each Saturday from noon in order to clean their sties. Similar measures were applied to dogs wandering in the city—but certain dogs such as greyhounds, spaniels and dogs used for sports were excepted.

2.  Order of 12 June 1368 (from the Old Free Book) allowing the church of St Peter Mancroft to enlarge its cemetery to take in part of the Market Place. The property consists of two lanes and a piece of vacant land. One lane,

called the Lindraperierowe had drapers' stalls on the south side and stalls of the worstedrow and spicerisrowe on the north side. The other lane had stalls 'late called the draperierowe' on both sides. Both lanes adjoined the common market at their east ends. The piece of empty land was at the west end of the lanes.

## 2. CHURCH RECORDS

There are several classes of record showing how the church was affected by the Black Death—appointments of clergymen, records of monastic houses, visitation records, and wills.

### Appointments of clergymen

The diocese of Norwich covered the whole of Norfolk and Suffolk. The annual average of episcopal institutions in diocese as a whole in the years before the Black Death was 81. In the single year 25 March 1349 to 24 March 1350 the number of institutions was 831. This equates to a mortality rate of 48.8%, joint highest of the English dioceses with Exeter and Winchester: some dioceses were rather lower, especially York at 39%. Christopher Harper-Bill improves on these figures: the average in the five years before 1349 was 77. In 1349, 800 parishes lost their incumbents, 83 of them twice, ten of them three times.

There was quite a high turnover in Norwich itself in the plague months. The situation is complicated because not all new appointments appear in the Bishop's register. Phyllis Pobst says that 20 parishes in the city, and possibly 24, were *donatives* - 'preferment was made to these by the patrons, without presentation to the bishop': so these would not be recorded in the episcopal records.

Presentations to Norwich parishes between June and December 1349:

| | |
|---|---|
| June: | Augustine, Michael at Plea, |
| July | Stephen, Edward, Swithin, Lawrence |
| August | Augustine (again), All Saints |
| October | Margaret, Lawrence (again), Botolph |
| December | Michael in King Street, Mary Unbrent |

Churches which were not donatives, but where there was no change of incumbent between June and December 1349: Peter Mancroft, Peter Southgate, Andrew, John Maddermarket, Peter Parmentergate, George Tombland, Clement, Edward, Mary Coslany, Michael Coslany. Thus about half of the parishes in Norwich that appear in the episcopal registers appointed new incumbents in the second half of 1349—two of them made two appointments.[6]

For comparison, I have looked at the same period in the previous year: there was not a single new appointment to a Norwich parish in the Bishop's register in the months June to December 1348, so clearly something unusual was happening in the city in 1349.

The bishop at the time of the Black Death was Bishop Bateman. He was conducting peace negotiations in France. On his return, he landed at Yarmouth on 10 June, when the plague was raging in his diocese: he was told that his brother, Sir Bartholomew Bateman of Gillingham, was dead. He returned to Norwich but then retreated to his rural palace at Hoxne, where he stayed until the plague was over.

## Monastic houses in Norwich

### St Mary in the fields

*Norwich St Andrew: the Dance of Death.*

This was a college of priests on the site of the present Assembly House. There were six prebends and no less than four new appointments to these positions had to be made July 1349. One of these was himself replaced in October. This is clear evidence of a high mortality rate in this college.

### Norwich Cathedral

There is evidence that there were about 65 monks in all in 1348, half of whom died in the plague. Numbers took time to rise, but there were over 50 again by the 1360s.

The figures are based on the St Leonard's cell account rolls: the cell paid a small sum as pocket money to each monk. H W Saunders, who researched the Cathedral account rolls, says that the figure dropped from an unknown number before the Black Death to 37. (He says that the sum paid in 1353-4 was £4, which is eighty shillings. The customary payment was two shillings a monk, but he thinks it likely that the prior took the share of four monks, hence his total of 37 monks). Sixty eight shillings were paid to the convent in 1354-5 and 98 shillings in 1373.

However, the Cathedral officials appear not to have succumbed at such a rate: Saunders points out that nine of the ten obedientiaries lived through the Black Death, the only exception being Ralph de Swanton.[7]

The accounts of the communar and pitancer also reveal evidence of crisis.

They record that building work on the cloisters comes to a sudden end on 25 June 1349, stone is sold and the remaining cash is divided between the obedientiaries for safe keeping. Tradition says that the north-west corner had been reached and that the mouldings in the arches here, which are of wood not of stone, are temporary ones put in at the time of the Black Death, and never replaced!

*The north-west corner Norwich Cathedral cloister has wooden rather than stone tracery.*

The account rolls of the infirmarer also suggest a time of chaos. Ralph de Swanton starts account in the normal way at Michaelmas 1348. John de Hedersett takes over on 10 July 1349, receiving from Alexander de Castre the sum of £27.10s, in gold and silver—including counterfeit money. His account records a profit of over £23, of which 52s 1d had been stolen! Ralph de Swanton may have died in the plague—he was an elderly man, having been a student at Oxford in about 1310.

*Norwich Cathedral cloister showing detail of the temporary wooden tracery.*

He was infirmarer from 1345, and was clearly sick as he charged the infirmary account for medicines for his own use each year. John de Heders survived the plague, being still alive in 1356-7.[8]

### Carrow Priory

The Bishop's register also records new appointments as head of monastic houses (friaries are not included). In the normal course of events there were about two of these in a year, but the numbers suddenly shoot up in 1349 with eleven new appointments in the single month of July 1349. Causes of death are not given but most, perhaps all, were presumably plague victims. They include Cicely de Plumstead at Carrow Priory, a house of Benedictine nuns just outside the city walls of Norwich. She was replaced as prioress by one of the other nuns, Alice de Hethersett. As records were only kept of heads of houses, we have no way of knowing how many other nuns may have died, let alone servants and guests there. At least the priory was not as badly hit as the small monastic house at Mountjoy in Haveringland, nine miles south of Norwich: the prior and all the canons died, and a new man had to be brought in from another Norfolk monastic house to be prior.

### The friaries

Friars are groups of men dedicated to helping the spiritual life of the poor. We might expect them to be especially active among those in poverty, and therefore at risk of catching the plague, and later tradition does associate high mortality rates with several groups of Norwich friars.

The Dominican or blackfriars were based at the complex now known as The Halls. In 1349, William of Blofield, a brother at the Carmelite friary in Cambridge (his name indicates he was a Norfolk man), wrote to a brother at the Dominican friary in Norwich describing rumours going the rounds in Rome:

> There are various prophets in the regions around Rome, whose identity is still secret, who have been making up stories like this for years. They say that this very year, 1349, Antichrist is aged ten, and is a most beautiful child, so well educated in all branches of knowledge that no one now living can equal him. And they also say that there is another boy, now aged twelve and living beyond the land of the Tartars, who has been brought up as a Christian and that this is he who will destroy the Saracens and become the greatest man in Christendom, but his power will be quickly brought to an end by the coming of Antichrist.
>
> These prophets also say, among a great deal else, that the present pope will come to a violent end, and that after his death there will be more revolutions in the world that there have ever been before. But after that another pope will arise, a good and just man, who will appoint God-fearing cardinals, and there will be almost total peace in his time. And after him there will be no other pope, but Antichrist will come and reveal himself.'[9]

There were at least fifty Dominicans in Norwich before the plague struck. David Knowles, in his seminal *The Religious Orders in England*, says 'we are told that the Norwich house of preachers was emptied to the last friar', and Christopher Harper-Bill, citing Knowles as his source, puts the same thing another way: 'the Norwich Dominicans were wiped out almost to a man'. Knowles' own source is given as *Victoria County History* vol 2 p.241. This source takes the information back to Tanner's eighteenth century *Notitia Monastica*: 'every one of the Dominican friars of Norwich died, so that their house was left empty and deserted'.[10]

However, the mortality is not mentioned in Helen Sutermeister's booklet on the Norwich Blackfriars, so presumably not in the articles by Palmer in *The*

*Norwich Dominican friary.*

*Reliquary* that she cites (I have not been able to find these articles). Nor is it mentioned in Wllliam A Hinnebusch's exhaustive book on the early English Dominican friaries, *The early English Friars Preachers*, (1951): perhaps 'early' does not extend into the mid-fourteenth century.

Interestingly, Edward Hutton thinks that the *Franciscans* in Norwich suffered: 'in Norwich the whole community seems to have perished'. This friary was at the top of what is now Prince of Wales Road: nothing of it now remains.[11]

However, mortality among the Norwich Franciscans is not mentioned in the works by J H Moorman on the history of the Franciscan Order, and on the Order in England., nor in A G Little's *Studies in English Franciscan History* (1917).

Francis Blomefield, writing in the eighteenth century, has a similar tradition for yet another group of friars, those of the Order of Our Lady, living in a house adjoining St Julian's churchyard. He says they 'continued here until Edward the Third's times and then dying in the great pestilence, their house afterwards became a private property'. Given these small orders of friars were forbidden to take new members in 1275, would there have been such a group in existence in 1349?

The seventeenth century Irish Franciscan writer, Wadding, thought the decline of the standards of the friars came as a result of the Black Death:

The evil wrought great destruction to the holy houses of religion carrying off the masters of regular discipline and the seniors of experience. From this time the monastic orders and in particular the mendicants, began to grow tepid and negligent both in that piety and that learning in which they had up to that time flourished.

Edward Hutton puts it in exceptionally forceful language:

it brought evil in its train; for, largely, those friars who survived the Death were the scum and refuse of the Order, those who had refused the service of the sick, those who had fled, the selfish and the fearful.... The strength and splendour of the Order, the flower of the friars died in the by-ways in that appalling catastrophe, the wasters remained to carry on the convents now enriched almost alone in a stricken world and wholly forgetful of the poverty of St Francis.[12]

## The evidence of wills

Wills are a key source for medieval attitudes towards death. Unfortunately, wills for Norwich Consistory court only survive from 1370, so there is no complete series of wills from the time of the Black Death. A very few wills of Norwich people do survive for the year 1349: two among the private title deeds already mentioned and two more in other archives of the city.

These four wills follow a common medieval pattern. The testator leaves his soul to God and some chosen saints, chooses a place of burial, makes religious bequests intended to help secure the salvation of the soul, and then makes bequests of property. These are actual people dying in Norwich during the Black Death of 1349, so their evidence is important.

1.  Will of John de Hanalbre de Martham of St Martin at Palace: wants to be buried in St Martin at Palace church and leaves money for the altar there. He made his will on 28 March, and it was proved on 20 April, so John died within a very short time of making his will. Presumably he was an incomer to the city from the Broadland village of Martham.

2.  Will of Thomas de Welborne, taverner and citizen. He asks for his body to be buried wherever his executors decide, and makes bequests to St Peter Mancroft and St Mary in the Fields in Norwich, and also to Welborne parish church. His name and the bequest to the church there strongly suggest he has come to the city from Welborne. He made his will on 23 May 1349, and it was proved just five days later. Had the spread of plague brought on the awareness of mortality, and was it the plague that killed him? We can never know for sure.

3.  Will of Millicent the widow of Thomas de Hemsby. She asks to be buried in the cemetery of the Great Hospital, and bequeaths her messuage in nearby Holme Street to named individuals. She made her will on 10 May 1349.

4.  Will of Nicholas de Kirkeby, proved in August 1349 at the time the Black Death was at its height in Norwich. He also asks to be buried in the cemetery of the Great Hospital, leaves money to it and to the church of St John in Ber Street.

These four make up the only wills that survive from the city made in the plague year of 1349. Three have names suggesting they are incomers to the city, and the fourth is the widow of a man with a name suggesting this: obviously it is too small a sample to be of significance, but it is an indication of the number of people in the city who were incomers even before the devastating effects of the Black Death.

## Inventory of Church Goods, 1368

This is held in the National Archives, but has been transcribed for the Norfolk Record Society and some entries refer to the plague. At St Matthew on Holme Street, the entry refers to a time 'in the year 1349 and before the pestilence'. The church has become ruinous by 1368, and the parishioners now go to St Martin [at Palace]. The entry for St Winwaloy lists the ornaments found there at the previous visitation 'before the plague'. The church became a chapelry attached to Carrow Priory and was finally demolished in the sixteenth century. The entry for St Olave (near the present flyover across Magdalen Street) makes no actual mention of the plague, but it seems there is no longer a population to support the church, as in July 1360 the Archdeacon placed its ornaments under the care of a parishioner and of the infirmarer of Norwich cathedral priory as the rector.

## Other sources

The Bishop of Norwich was granted a *dispensation* in October 1350 to allow 60 clerks who had passed their 20th birthdays to hold rectories: the canonical age was 25. Bateman established Trinity Hall Cambridge in 1350: in the *foundation deed* it was specifically laid down that the purpose of the new college was to make good the appalling losses which the clergy in England, and in particular East Anglia, had suffered. According to Harper-Bill, 'In Norwich diocese 29 *unifications of benefices* are recorded from 1349 onwards, whereas there had been only four in the early fourteenth century.'[13]

## Architecture

The change of architectural style from Decorated to Perpendicular may have been stimulated by the Black Death in Norwich as elsewhere. Lindley writes:

According to John Harvey, regional differences in the effects of the Black Death may account for the fact that so many royal masons of the second half of the century, such as Henry Yeverley, John Palterton and Simon Roucestere, were of north midlands origin, filling the vacuum left by the deaths of East Anglian masons such as the Ramseys.

However, Harvey himself was sure it was not the Black Death that led to the rise of the Perpendicular style of architecture. He thinks that 'the essentials of the perpendicular had been laid down by William Ramsey before his death in 1349' and specifically states that 'it is important to realise that its [the perpendicular style] origins had nothing whatever to do with the Black Death, so commonly invoked by those who would have us believe that the perpendicular style is the product of penury and a shortage of skilled craftsmen'. However, he agrees that the Black Death killed many of the earlier architects, allowing the younger ones new opportunities. The

*A church in Norwich lost because of the Black Death.*

many Perpendicular style churches in Norwich today are possibly a direct, and certainly an indirect, consequence of the Black Death. The Ramseys were working on Norwich Cathedral cloisters when they died in 1349.[14]

## 3. THE SUBURBS

The city of Norwich covered the area within its walls, approximately that of the Inner Ring Road. The many suburban areas that make up modern Norwich were then villages in the countryside. Descriptions of the plague in Norwich do not normally take in these areas, but, as they are where nearly everyone in Norwich now lives, I have looked at the effects of the plagues in these areas as well. For the Black Death, the main sources are manor court rolls. I have looked at those manors that are now suburbs, Eaton and Trowse.

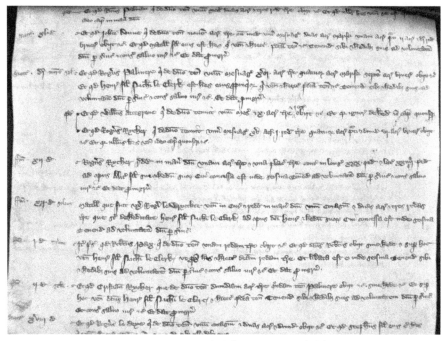

*Eaton manor court 1349 (NRO, DCN 60/9/3).*

The manor court records for **Eaton** show the devastating effect of the Black Death on a village outside Norwich, now a city suburb. The last court held before the Black Death was on 13 December 1348. By the time the next court is held on St Mary's Day (could be 8 or 20 July) 1349, there has been an upheaval within the manor. A new tenant is required for 25 different family holdings. A surviving tenant is giving up his property in just two cases, and in one of these there may have been a recent death: Matilda, once the wife of Roger le Wryeche comes to the court to surrender the land: it is purchased by Henry, son of Nicholas le Clerk, of whom we shall hear more in a moment. In all the other 23 cases, the tenant has died. The next of kin now comes to the court and makes a claim as heir. This would normally be the eldest surviving son, but in only four cases does a son come forward: one such person is Thomas Western as son and heir of his deceased father, Richard Western. In all the other cases, either a more distant relative comes, or there is no heir at all. Of these nineteen cases, in three cases a daughter comes forward, in one case with her mother: perhaps the daughter was under age. In three other cases, there are no surviving children and a brother of the deceased tenant comes forward as nearest surviving heir: in one of these cases, the land was held jointly by two sisters, Agnes and Emma, as daughters of Reginald Attetownsend: both have died and William, their brother, comes as heir. In seven further cases, the heir is a more distant relative:

1. Margaret the daughter of Robert Pax and Agnes his sister held one

property jointly. Both are dead. Matilda the daughter of Simon Pax and 'of the same blood' as the deceased woman comes forward as heir.

2. John Golden has died. Thomas, the son of his daughter Matilda comes forward.

3. Christian Richer has died. William Attetownsend 'of the same blood' comes forward.

4. Julian Pax has died. Matilda, daughter of Simon Pax, and aunt of the said Julian comes forward—again!

5. William Attechurch has died. Julian the son of William's sister Margaret comes forward.

6. Roger Palmer has died. Henry, son of Nicholas le Clerk, comes forward as heir—what his relationship was to Roger is not stated.

7. Ralph, son of Thomas Attetownsend, has died. His heir is Emma, the sister of Thomas and aunt of Ralph. However, she does not come to court to state her claim so that the land goes into the hands of the lord of the manor.

In nine cases, not far short of half of the total, we are told that there are no heirs. In all these cases the land would eventually revert to the lord, but in two cases he immediately finds a new tenant, who in both instances is the aforesaid Henry, son of Nicholas le Clerk: we are unequivocally told that he is NOT the heir in either case. In the case of William Attegreene, it is recorded that 'no one knows of an heir'. Other instances simply say 'no heirs', or in the case of Roger Richer 'no heirs come'.[15]

This gives us a flavour of a manor just outside Norwich, now a Norwich suburb, in the time of the Black Death, and hints at winners as well as losers. Matilda, the daughter of Simon Pax, has inherited two properties that she would probably not have gained in other circumstances, and Henry, son of Nicholas le Clerk, has gained greatly by a mixture of inheritance and entry into lands left vacant.

The next court was held on 28 October and involved some tidying up of loose ends. Thomas Western has already died, and now his brother John Western inherits the property, having lost his father and his eldest brother in a very short time. William Attetownsend now comes forward as being heir and of the same blood as William Attegreene, so that the jury were right to be cautious in this case. More surprisingly Thomas Richer now comes to the court and claims as Roger Richer's son and heir: perhaps he was a younger son and had left the manor not expecting to inherit but now claims the family inheritance.

Similar events took place at **Trowse**, for which the earliest surviving manorial court roll is for 30 October 1349: the lack of earlier rolls may itself be a result of the confusion caused by the Black Death. Again, the record catches the process of tidying up after a disaster. Heirs now come forward claiming pieces of land which had passed into the hands of the lord as no claimant had turned up at the previous court, and others pass out of the families concerned as there is no heir to inherit.

1.  Simon Ode had died in occupation of a messuage, seven acres of land and one acre of meadow. His daughter and heir, Agnes, is just one year old: we are told that she did not turn up(!)—the tenancy therefore passes out of the family. The new tenant is Richard Turnecurt.

2.  John Hert died in occupation of a cottage. It is now claimed by Agnes as daughter of his sister Margaret and his nearest living heir.

3.  John Wreton died in occupation of a small piece of land. He has no surviving heirs so the land escheated to the lord of the manor, who now grants it to Roger Wrorer.

4.  William Eem has died and his brother Richard has also died. The land is now jointly claimed by Juliana and Isabella, the daughters of William, and John, the son of Katherine. The clerk's genealogical knowledge seems to have failed him here: there is much erasing in the relevant entries, Katherine being described once as the sister of William and once as the daughter of Richard!

5.  Thomas Chapman has died. Annabella, the daughter of Thomas de Dunham, comes and claims as heir: the relationship is not stated.

6.  Letitia le Smyth died in possession of a cottage. She had no heirs, so the lord now grants it to Warin Ambelour.

7.  John Crom died in possession of a messuage and four acres of land. Cecilia de Hindringham comes to the court and gives it to the use of William de Acle. Any relationship between Crom and Cecilia is not stated.

8.  The final entry at this court concerns Richard de Lakenham, palfreyman: he has died and his son Gilbert comes forward to claim as heir. The lord and his clerk must have been pleased to set down this entry, the only 'normal' case of succession among the eight![16]

Other manors suffered in a similar way, as the financial records show. According to Saunders, receipts from the manor court at **Catton** fell from £15 in 1348-9 to just £3. 5s in 1349-40. At **Taverham**, he says, twelve tenants out of 25 were dead, only five leaving sons or daughters.[17]

I have chosen these examples as being very close to Norwich, but similar stories can be extracted from manor court rolls all over the county. The mortality at Hakeford Hall manor in Coltishall, just seven miles north of Norwich, has been estimated by Bruce Campbell to be as high as 70% taking the 1349 and subsequent outbreaks together. A few miles further west at Kirk Hall manor in Salle, there were about seventy tenants: 46 deaths were recorded at the first court held after 25 March 1349, and fourteen more in October of the same year. In eleven cases no heirs could be found, and the land reverted to the lord of the manor. Further research among Norfolk's manor court rolls would show which Norfolk villages were spared and which were especially badly hit.[18]

## SUBURBAN CLERGYMEN

New clergymen were appointed at **Earlham** on 5 May and 19 July 1349. There was one new appointment at **Eaton** on 18 June 1349. As with the clergymen in the city, we have no way of knowing that the vacancies were caused by deaths from plague, but the need for two appointments at Earlham in ten weeks could suggest at least one Black Death fatality here. This may not seem a very high proportion of deaths in the parishes around Norwich: however, it must be remembered that many of the parishes—Costessey, Cringleford, Lakenham, Sprowston, Trowse and Thorpe St Andrew—were either donatives or peculiars, so that any new appointments of clergymen to these churches would not appear in the Bishop's register.

## AFTERWARDS

We have little idea of what the population of the city was immediately after the Black Death. There is no actual record of what the population of Norwich was until the poll tax of 1377, when there had been at least two further devastating outbreaks of plague in the city. Historian Carole Rawcliffe says, 'the poll tax returns for 1377, which were supposed to record all individuals over the age of fourteen except for beggars and members of religious orders, list a mere 3952 names for Norwich. Even allowing for omissions and evasions, the entire population was then unlikely to have exceeded 8,000, and was probably much lower.' Ziegler says that the Norwich Poll tax figure in 1377 equates to a population of 5,928.[19]

### Notes

1    Jim Bolton, 'The World Turned Upside Down' in Ormrod and Lindley, *The Black Death in England* (1996) p.23; P Lindley, The Black Death in English Art' in *op. cit.* p.141.

2    Elizabeth Rutledge, 'Immigration and population growth in early fourteenth century Norwich: evidence from the tithing roll', *Urban History Yearbook* (1988), pp.5-30; ibid, 'Norwich before the Black Death' in Rawcliffe and Wilson editors, *Medieval Norwich* (2004) p.158.

3  Philip Ziegler, *The Black Death* (1970 edition) p.173, Horrox *op. cit.* p.63;AntoniaGransden (editor), 'A fourteenth century chronicle from the Grey Friars at Lynn, *English Historical Review* LXXII, 1957, p.274.

4  William Hudson and J C Tingey, *Records of the City of Norwich*, vol II page cxxi.

5  Penny Dunn, 'Trade, Norwich before the Black Death' in Rawcliffe and Wilson editors, *Medieval Norwich* (2004) pp.213-4.

6  Ziegler, *op. cit.* p.177; C Harper-Bill, 'English Religion after the Black Death' in Ormrod and Lindley *op. cit.* p.85; Phyllis Pobst, (editor), *The Register of Bishop Bateman* (1996 and 2000), *passim*. The original register is in the Norfolk Record Office.

7  H W Saunders, *An introduction to the account rolls of Norwich Cathedral Priory* (1930) p.186.

8  Norfolk Record Office (hereafter NRO), DCN 1/10/7.

9  quoted in Horrox, *op. cit.* p.154.

10  Christopher Harper-Bill, 'English Religion after the Black Death' in Ormrod and Lindley, *The Black Death in England* (1996) p.97.He cites David Knowles, *The Religious Orders in England* (1951) volume II pp.10-11.

11  Edward Hutton, *The Franciscans in England* (1926) p.177.

12  Quoted in Hutton *op. cit.* p.180.

13  Christopher Harper-Bill, 'English Religion after the Black Death' in Ormrod and Lindley, *op. cit.* p.93; Ziegler *op. cit.* p.262.

14  P Lindley, 'The Black Death and English Art' in Ormrod and Lindley, *op. cit.* p.141.

15  NRO, DCN 60/9/3.

16  NRO, DCN 20/27/8.

17  Saunders *op. cit.* p.189.

18  Bruce Campbell, 'Population pressure, inheritance and the land market in a fourteenth century peasant community' in R M Smith (ed) *Land, kinship and life-cycle* (1984) pp.87-134; W L E Parsons *Salle* (1937) p.107.

19  Carole Rawcliffe, 'Sickness and Health', in Rawcliffe and Wilson editors, *Medieval Norwich* (2004) p.319; Ziegler *op. cit.* p.176.

# Plague Between 1349 and 1579

THE plague died away in Britain in the autumn of 1349 and prayers of thanksgiving were offered. However, it had not gone away for good. There were to be second, third and many more waves, of differing intensity and varying over the country, for the next 300 years.

The Lynn Grey Friars' chronicle says, 'in 1361 there was a great pestilence in the south of England, with the death of children and adolescents and of the wealthy'. The pestilence was considerably less than that of thirteen years earlier: nevertheless, it must have been pretty bad as it was known as 'the second pestilence'.[1]

Carole Rawcliffe says there were also outbreaks in Norwich in 1369 (a year which again saw a sharp rise in the number of men invited to become freemen), and in 1383. An anonymous chronicler writes of the 1369 outbreak: 'it was great beyond measure, lasted a long time and was particularly fatal to children.' Mostyn John Armstrong, the eighteenth century historian gives the date of the second outbreak as 1382, in which year, he says, 'a very pestilential fever broke out in many parts of the county'.

There was yet another spike or wave in 1390–1. The chronicler Thomas Walsingham wrote that 'such a mortality arose in Norfolk and in many other counties that it was thought as bad as the great pestilence'. Armstrong says that:

> a great mortality at this time broke out, which lasted twelve months, occasioned by the people's eating unwholesome food; and this not so much from a scarcity of corn as of money to purchase it: it raged greatly in Norfolk and many other counties, and was nearly in degree equal to the great pestilence.[2]

It is intriguing that three important religious writers in Norfolk must have experienced outbreaks of plague during their childhoods. Julian of Norwich was born in 1342, so would have been about seven at the time of the Black Death. Some books speculate that this had an important influence on her thinking. Richard Caister, vicar of St Stephen's in Norwich and writer of a popular prayer, was born in about 1360, and Margery Kempe, King's Lynn pilgrim and author, in about 1373. Too young for the first outbreak, they would have lived through those of the 1380s and 1390s.[3]

The Paston letters have several references to plague in the later fifteenth century. In 1454, William Paston in London wrote back to his brother John: 'here is great pestilence.' In a letter written probably on 10 November 1465, John Wymondham wrote from Norwich to his cousin John Paston that there was a child dead and another dying 'at Astley's': Wymondham and his wife had therefore asked John's wife to come and stay with them. Margaret Paston's mother and cousin fled Norwich in 1465 because the plague 'was so fervent in Norwych', and the family deserted the city again in 1471 for the same reason. Writing on 14 September 1471 from Waltham next Winchester, to his younger brother (confusingly also called John) Sir John Paston says,

> I pray you send me word if any of our friends or well-willers be dead, for I fear that there is great death in Norwich and in other borough towns in Norfolk. For I ensure you it is the most universal death that I ever wist in England; for, by my troth, I cannot hear by pilgrims that pass the country that any borough town in England is free from that sickness. God ceases it when it pleaseth Him.

He suggested self-isolation to protect his younger brothers: their mother was to take care that they did not go anywhere where the plague was raging and did not mix with other young people 'which resorteth where any sickness is'.

On 5 November 1471, Margaret Paston, in a letter to her son John in London, names some people who have died (presumably of plague), including 'Picard the baker of Tombland', and two women simply described as 'Veal's wife' and 'London's wife'. She does not actually say they were plague victims, but they presumably were as she continues: 'all this household and this parish is as you left it, blessed be God. We live in fear, but wot not whither to flee, for to be better than we be here.'

Armstrong says that the plague raged furiously throughout England in 1477 but does not specifically mention Norwich. However, he records that in the following year:

> In 1478, the latter end of September, another broke out; and continued its ravages till November 1479; in which time, according to Neville's account, there died an incredible number of people in this city.

Indeed, the only direct reference to a plague in Norwich that I have found in the official records of the city between 1349 and 1579 is for 1479, in the 'Mayor's Book', compiled 50 years after the event. To a list of officials for 1479 has been added the words: 'This year was a great plague within the city of Norwich'.[4]

Again we have the evidence of the Paston letters. John Paston wrote from

Norwich in 1479: 'the people die sore in Norwich, and especially about my house, by my wife and my woman come not ought, and flee further we cannot, for at Swainsthorpe since my departing thence, they have died and been sick in every house in the town'. Swainsthorpe is a small village five miles south of Norwich: the Pastons owned a manor there.

In October 1479, Sir John Paston was in London on business, writing home: 'for the first four days I was in such fear of the sickness, and also found my chamber and stuff not so clean as I deemed, which troubled me sore'. By December, he was more relaxed: 'Thanked be God, the sickness is well ceased here'. He added a comment that people in lockdowns in later centuries can relate to: 'and also my business putteth away fear.' The psychological importance of not allowing the mind to dwell on the dangers was recognised even then.

There was a further serious outbreak in Norwich in 1544, 'during which' according to Carole Rawcliffe, 'the mortality rate appears to have more than trebled'. Alexander Neville, the chronicler of Kett's Rebellion, noted that the 1544 outbreak was especially bad in Norwich. It led to concern about the unhealthiness of some dwellings in the city due to overcrowding: 'much people in a small room living uncleanly and sluttishly'.[5] The city was also suffering from the aftermath of a severe flood that damaged cockeys (streams, the word appears to be unique to Norwich) and streets. Cartloads of refuse were piled up in several places; at Westwick Gates the piles prevented people passing through, while the city ordered that similar piles be removed from the Market Place when they heard of an impending visit by the Duke of Norfolk. In 1548, alderman Edmund Wood gave money to help clean up the city: the river was dredged, and four extra carts were bought to help in removing 'filthie and vile mater' from the streets.[6]

Despite these efforts, there was a

*The boom towers: a chain across the river could prevent boats entering the city in time of plague.*

further outbreak in the city in 1554-5. Paul Slack picked this up from burials in parish registers, which began being kept in 1538 (although only a relatively small number survive from that date). He thinks that 'the chronological distribution of burials indicates that both (1544 and 1554 outbreaks) were outbreaks of plague'. Parish registers survive for this date for ten city parishes, and they show a burial rate for both 1544 and 1554 as about three times the usual number. Slack gives the plague years in Norwich as 1485, 1500, 1513-4, 1520, 1544-5, 1554-5, 1557-9.[7]

People with business or other interests were naturally concerned as to how bad plague was elsewhere: contemporary correspondence frequently contains mention of the disease. Letters addressed to Nathaniel Bacon at Cockthorpe and Stiffkey on the north Norfolk coast, for example, included references to the plague being 'scattered in many places' in 1573, being present at Royston and Cambridge in 1575, and being in the camp of the Spanish army in 1577, the latter reference being sent by Nathaniel's brother Edward in Geneva.[8]

A dramatic reminder of the fear that the plague caused can still be seen in one Norfolk church. A parishioner wrote a desperate message on the wall of the chancel in Acle church; it is in Latin, but reads in translation; 'Take note, Oh too gloomy death, how many you are drowning in the depths. Death you snatch away now these, now these, now people everywhere'. It also refers to the vanity of ladies wearing horned head-dresses, which, according to the art historian Nikolaus Pevsner, suggests the reference is not to the Black Death of 1349 but a fifteenth century outbreak when these were in fashion.[9]

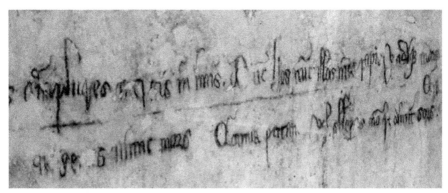

*Part of the graffito scrawled on to the north wall of St. Edmund's church, Acle.*

Of course, there were other diseases apart from the plague, and these could also have a great mortality. One was the influenza epidemic of 1558-9: no less than ten out of the 24 aldermen died—'the loss of such a large proportion of the city's governors was unprecedented'.[10]

## Notes

1   Horrox, *op. cit.* p.86.

2   Rawcliffe, 'Sickness and Health', in Rawcliffe and Wilson, *op. cit.* p.318.

3   For Caister, see Frank Meeres, *The life of Richard Caister the good vicar* (2020). Veronica Mary Rolf has a brilliantly imaginative account of how the Black Death may have affected Julian in *Julian's Gospel* (2013).

4   NRO, NCR 17b, The Mayor's Book p.14.

5   Carole Rawcliffe, *Medicine for the soul, the life, death and resurrection of an English medieval hospital* (1999) p.206.

6   Isla Faye, *The Norwich River and Street Accounts*, Norfolk Record Society vol LXXVII (2013) p.108.

7   Paul Slack, *The Impact of Plague in Tudor and Stuart England* (1991) p.127.

8   *Papers of Nathaniel Bacon*, Norfolk Record Society volume 46 (1978-9) pp.99, 174; volume 49 (1982-3), p.10.          ·

9   Nikolaus Pevsner and Bill Wilson, *The Buildings of England—Norfolk 1* (1997) pp.357-8.

10  Muriel McClendon, *The Quiet Reformation* (1999) p.195.

*Burial register, St. Michael at Plea, 1579 (NRO, PD 66/1).*

# The Crisis Years, 1579 to 1603

## THE PLAGUE OUTBREAK OF 1579

B Y the early 1500s, people were beginning to fight back, introducing measures designed to prevent an outbreak of plague, or at least to limit its spread. Some attempts had been made from the very beginning—when plague was in Bristol in 1349, the city authorities in Gloucester attempted to apply a local lockdown by closing the gates to their city. The whole essence of Boccaccio's *Decameron* is that a group of wealthy young people are self-isolating in the countryside while plague is raging in the city of Florence: not having resources like Netflix, they entertain themselves by telling stories. 'Lockdown' and 'self-isolation' made their first appearances from the very start of the epidemic, although the actual terms were never used in those times.

In the sixteenth century, such measures came to be applied more systematically. Certain cities issued plague orders from the early sixteenth century onwards, beginning with London in 1518. In 1579/80 a set of orders was issued by the Privy Council, the monarch's advisory council, very broadly equivalent to today's Cabinet—except that it was directly responsible to the King or Queen (who was not bound to take its advice), unlike the present Cabinet which is responsible to Parliament. Parliament had no say in the 1579/80 plague orders.

There were seventeen orders in all, as follows (a summary in modern English):

1.  Justices of all counties are to assemble at a place free of infection to consult on how these orders may be executed.

2.  First, justices should inquire as to which towns and villages are infected; then, how many are infected; and what wealth there is in each town to help determine how to relieve the poor who are infected. Finally, those infected should be confined to their houses.

3.  Then the justices should make a taxation within each infected town; by charging either one gross sum for all persons or by charging only special persons of wealth. If that amount is not sufficient, then justices are to extend taxation to adjoining places or towns.

4.  Justices must appoint persons to view bodies of those who die so that before the burial they may certify to the minister and churchwarden of what disease those persons died. Also, justices must pay a weekly

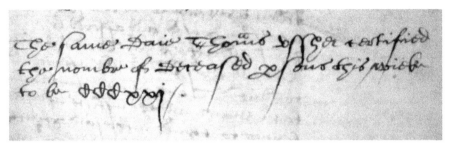

*Certificate of burials before the Mayor's Court, 1579 (NRO, 16a/10).*

allowance to those who perform this service. Persons chosen are sworn to make a true report. The choice of persons should be made by the curate of the church along with three or four substantial men of the parish. If those chosen refuse to serve, or give false testimony, imprison them as a lesson to others.

5.     If someone dies of plague or it is known someone is sick with it, shut up his house for five weeks after sickness has ceased or the person has died. In towns, adjoining houses must be shut in the same manner. If in the country, those who are ill, or those from houses of the ill, even if they must leave their houses to care for their animals or their crops, must refrain from going into the company of others, except wearing a mark on their clothes or bearing white rods if they go abroad. Justices should appoint night watchmen to see that infected houses do not allow persons in or out. Punishment for disobedience is the stocks. Special marks are to be fitted on the doors of infected houses. When infection occurs at inns and ale houses, signs are to be removed and crosses or a mark set up in place, as a token of the sickness.

6.     Justices should choose honest persons to collect tax and take care of poor sick, providing them with food, fire and medicine.

7.     Justices should appoint persons to take food and necessities to the sick— they must wear a mark or carry rods to identify themselves.

8.     In each town justices should make provisions for preservatives and remedies bespoke and made to be distributed without great cost.

9.     Ministers and churchwardens must report each week the number of the sick that do not die and the number who do die. These deaths and causes should be certified to the rest of the justices of the assembly. This information must be kept in a special book.

10.     Justices should appoint a place in each parish for burial. Bury the dead after sunset.

11. Justices of the whole county are to meet every 21 days to see whether these orders are duly executed and must notify the Privy Council of what they find.

12. Justices in the hundred [a district or part of a county] are to meet once a week where any infection is, to see if orders are being followed. They are to take problems into their own hands or report them to the general assembly.

13. After anyone dies of plague, all clothes and bedding are to be burned or handled as physicians require in the Advices.

14. If the justices devise new directives, they must be set in writing and distributed. If anyone knowingly disobeys, they will be imprisoned or made known to the Queen and/or her Privy Council.

15. If there is a lack of justices, none need be appointed.

16. If any ecclesiastical or lay person says or writes that it is uncharitable to forbid the visiting of the infected, pretending no person shall die until his time, such persons shall be apprehended; and if in ecclesiastical orders, he shall be forbidden to preach; if lay, he shall be forbidden to utter such dangerous opinions on pain of imprisonment.

17. Justices need take great care because without these directives plague may increase.

## Norwich

1579 is not on Eric Wood's list of main outbreaks of plague in England, but in Norwich it was a terrible year.[1] The wave of plague in 1579 was devastating in the city, more so than any outbreak apart from that of 1349. It is a reasonable guess that three or four out of ten of the population died within a few months— compare that figure with the death rates in 2020! We have two sources of record that give us a great deal more information on the plagues of the Tudor and Stuart period than those of the Middle Ages—the records of the Mayor's Court show what steps the authorities took to try to prevent the spread of the plague, while the surviving burial registers for the 34 parishes of the city give us the numbers—and, for the first time, the actual names—of those dying of plague. In later outbreaks, an increasing number of the parishes actually indicated those burials of plague victims (usually with the word 'plague' or the letter 'P' beside the entries). This was not done by anyone in 1579 (and some parish clerks never did it), so it is not possible from the registers to distinguish those who died from plague from those who died from other causes.

The Privy Council placed the responsibility for plague control on county

*Norwich in the later sixteenth century, by Braun and Hogenberg.*

Justices of the Peace. Norwich was a city and county in its own right and not part of Norfolk. It had its own Justices of the Peace—the current Mayor and those aldermen who had previously been Mayor.

The city was run by an Assembly consisting of aldermen and common council, but the day-to-day running was in the hands of the aldermen in the Mayor's Court. Norwich was divided into four Great Wards (Mancroft, Conesford, Wymer and North, also known as Over the Water, as it was made up of the area north of the river Wensum). There were twenty-four aldermen (and of course they *were* all men), six for each ward in the city. The Great Wards were subdivided into twelve Small or Petty Wards; two aldermen were assigned to each ward for which they were responsible. For example, when it was decided to count the number of 'Strangers' in the city in 1571, it was the aldermen who counted the number in each of the Small Wards. Once elected, a man would serve for the rest of his life, so that the same man might remain aldermen for ten twenty years, or even longer. You would know your aldermen, and the alderman would know what was going on within his ward.

The Mayor for the year was chosen from among the aldermen. He was elected on 1 May and held his first court on the second or third Wednesday in June. The Mayor's Court met every Wednesday and Saturday, sometimes even more often, and it was this body that decided what regulations were to apply and when and decided when it was the right time to ease them.

In all the examples I have looked at, the Mayor was present at his own court. The court was also normally attended by the sheriffs, who were both king's officers but also served the Mayor's warrants. There were two sheriffs, one chosen by the aldermen and the other elected by the Common Council: they served as sheriff for a year. They had to be freemen of the city and resident in Norwich. Some people chose not to be sheriff, and paid fairly hefty sums of money to get out of it, but for those who took up the position, it could be the start of a lifetime of service in city government.

*Order of the Mayor's Court, 1579 (NRO, NCR 16a/10).*

The aldermen came from a fairly limited pool of citizens: you had to serve as sheriff first. You also had to be someone of substance: I have not seen any exact definition of what this meant, but the Mayor could intervene if he thought someone was not of sufficient status. In any case, aldermen were not paid, so the position was restricted to those who could afford to give up two afternoons a week or more. What is more, on his election each alderman had to give forty shillings to the City Treasurer, theoretically to help maintain the city walls. This all meant that the aldermen came from the highest rank of citizens: most of them were merchants, grocers or mercers, others were substantial craftsmen and tradesmen. Of course, not all the aldermen regularly attended the court: in a typical year eight or ten might attend almost all the meetings, with the Mayor and one or both sheriffs almost always present. These were the men who ran the city and made the decisions about combatting plague.

Legally, the aldermen were of two kinds, and this was always noted in the Court records. The Mayor himself and all those aldermen who had spent a year as Mayor were Justices of the Peace, or magistrates as they are also called. These men had the legal powers to enforce the decisions of the Court. Those aldermen who had not served as Mayor did not have this status. Because aldermen served for life, most could

*Norwich Guildhall, where the Mayor and aldermen met at least twice a week.*

expect eventually to be Mayor: on average, about a third to a half of the aldermen at any given court were former mayors and therefore Justices.

In addition to the wards, the city was subdivided in another way, into ecclesiastical parishes. There had been over fifty churches in the medieval city but by the later sixteenth century it had been rationalised into 34 parishes, each centred round a medieval church: the enormous number of churches is one of the factors making Norwich such an attractive city. This church would be the centre of many activities: people would attend their church every Sunday (this was before the growth of Nonconformist churches). This is where decisions about isolating and lockdown made by the aldermen would be read out. The church or churchyard was the only place where one could be baptised, married and buried. In addition, the church raised rates to maintain the building and also to look after the poor living within the parish. When the aldermen needed to raise money to pay for the expenses of plague on the city, it was the parish overseers who actually collected the money—there are several instances of overseers being fined for failing to carry this out properly.

Norwich was exceptional in the large numbers of refuges who came to the city from the Low Countries from the 1560s onwards. They were Protestants fleeing religious persecution. Known in the city as 'the Strangers', the majority were Dutch speakers, but a significant number spoke French, also known as Walloons. At one time, there were at least 5,000 of these incomers, making up a quarter to a third of the inhabitants of Norwich (the population of the city is not known, 15,000 being a reasonable guess). The two groups had their own churches and were responsible for looking after the poor within their community.

Some books give the impression of a contrast between the recent incomers and the 'native' population, with the implication that most of the latter had lived in the city for centuries. This was very far from the case. Cities like Norwich had an enormously high mortality rate, plague being just one of the many diseases to strike in an overcrowded and unsanitary environment. The city could only survive, let alone increase in size, through an enormous number of incomers arriving for economic and social opportunities. Many of the inhabitants of the city would be incomers just as much as the Strangers, but from the Norfolk countryside rather than from abroad. It was these incomers that enabled the city to bounce back so quickly from the major upheavals caused by massive plague casualties in 1579, 1603 and 1665.

When there were signs of an outbreak of plague in March 1579, the first actions of the Mayor's Court were concerned not with the city as a whole but specifically with the Stranger community: any sudden crisis can easily lead to xenophobia. On 31 March, the City Assembly noted that plague had broken out, starting in St Stephen's and All Saints parishes. Some people were already blaming the incomers, on three grounds:

18. They scoured their bays [a type of cloth, a speciality of the Dutch incomers] in the river
19. They combed wool in open shops and poured the wash in the gutters, where it remained
20. They did not keep their 'necessaries' [toilets] in good order

The Mayor sent letters to the Dutch and Walloon communities ordering them to remedy these issues: no Stranger was to scour bays in the river between New Mills and Whitefriars Bridge; they were to use water to flush down the gutters into the steams; they were to keep their necessaries dry. The actual words recorded in the City Assembly book are:

The last day of March 1579. This day at an Assembly by reason of some infection begun in the city, whereupon the plague is partly already begun both at St Stephen's and All Saints parish, and for that at this Assembly was great complaints made against the Strangers for the corrupt keeping of their houses and necessaries, and also for the great annoyance of the river by scouring their bayes and washing them all along the river to the great infection of the same. And also for keaming [combing] of wool in open shops and carrying chamber wash through the city in the daytime, and for pouring out wash in their gutters, and not pouring water after it, whereby it resteth in the gutters and breedeth great infections, and of many other enormities like thereunto. And for the reformation thereof a law was made and a precept directed to them to redress the same, the contents whereof be as hereafter ensueth, viz:

BY THE MAYOR To the Ministers of the Dutch and Walloon congregations of the city of Norwich and to every of them: -

Whereas great complaints have been made to me and other my brethren and especially (generally) in a common Assembly held at the Guild Hall of the same city the last day of March last past part, that the scourers of your bays within the river of the same city dwelling along the whole river do so corrupt the same as the unwholesomeness of the water does not only poison the whole fish of the river, but also doth so poison the water that the corruption thereof (to such as of necessity are fain to occupy the same) doth breed in their bodies diverse corrupt humours to the great danger of their bodies in this infectious time. And forasmuch as by certain directions from Her Majesty and her honourable Council that all causes of infection should be removed from places needful: it is therefore enacted that no Stranger shall scour (in the river of this city from the New Mills to the bridge called Whitefriars Bridge) any manner of bayes, after the first of May next coming, upon the pain that for every baye so scoured they shall forfeit three shillings and four pence to the Mayor, the poor and the presenter. And further that no keamer [comber] of wool do keam their wool near to the street to the annoyance of the passers-by, nor shall cast out any scouring wash in the daytime when the people may gather infection, but to do the same in the night. And after their wash cast out, to cast after such quantity of water as the same shall not corrupt, but pass to the cockeys under the ground without the hurt of any person, upon like pain, and upon pain of imprisonment and other fine to be set upon them by the discretion of the Mayor and Justices.

Given the ninth day of April 1579—You have also to take good regard that your necessaries be kept dry without wash, for the wash corrupts and brings great infection, and use such cleansing of your houses, your clothes and bodies, and also use such fumes and preservatives as the physicians shall advise you, and as is set down (in print) to be used by Her Highness's commandment. Greatly foreseeing that if the plague begin among you that the persons infected come not abroad but be shut up according to the said orders, and to have their necessary food appointed them, and their keepers to do the like. And you the Ministers to certify to us how many do sicken of the plague or do die, and that daily, upon such pains as in the said orders be contained. And that all dogs (within such infected houses) be killed. and none at all be suffered to wander and stray from house to house, but to be kept tied at home at their several

*Sixteenth century houses in King Street.*

houses, upon like pain, imprisonment and fine as is aforesaid. Willing you the Ministers to publish these letters to your congregation for the better observing the same.

It is not obvious from the parish registers of All Saints and St Stephen's which, if any, people actually died of the plague around 30 March. At All Saints, after just one burial in the eight weeks from the beginning of February to 28 March, there was a 'spike' in the number of burials, with four in less than a week, between 30 March and 4 April. At the much larger parish of St Stephen's, there was also an increase in the number of burials at this time. The most likely plague victims are those families which lost several members in a very short time: two daughters of Edmund Brewster were buried on 31 March and 2 April, while Edward Lewington lost his wife and two sons, buried between 3 and 9 April.

This was the only meeting of the City Assembly during the 1579 outbreak: all other decisions were made in the Mayor's Court. It is possible that this body may have been less xenophobic than the Assembly with its 60 common councillors. All the actions of the Mayor's Court are directed to the inhabitants as a whole, none specifically concerned with the Stranger community. On 4 April, the Mayor's Court ordered that the wardens of the butchers' gild must warn both the city butchers and country butchers that they kill no flesh within the walls of the city during the time of plague.

The city authorities then took a new step to quantify the mortality in the city: Norwich appears to have been the first city in England to attempt this. On 26 June 1579, the court swore Thomas Usher, raffman, to certify the names of the deceased every week. From then the *numbers* (not the names in spite of the court's instruction) of burials are recorded: see Appendix Two. From the last week in October, there is a further fact recorded: the numbers of 'strangers' among the dead are noted. The burials from plague are not distinguished from other burials in the figures: this was to come later. The figures begin just in time to demonstrate the horrors of this particular outbreak of the plague. There were 56 burials in the first week, that ending on 27 June, and the figure rose inexorably to 244 in the week ending 1 August. There were well over 200 burials a week for fourteen successive weeks, peaking at 352 burials in the week ending 15 August, and continuing into the third week of October. The figures then fell throughout the rest of the year, to just under thirty a week at the year's end. There was no plague in the following week and the lowest possible number of burials was recorded on 15 June 1580, when it was noted, 'God be praised was but one [burial] which was an infant stranger'. The figures from October onwards show how high the mortality rate was among the strangers—up to 80% of burials regularly come from this community.

The aldermen were concerned with the financial aspects of the outbreak, especially the effect on the poor in the city. The aldermen agreed that the city had to take responsibility. At a Mayor's Court meeting on 1 July 1579 it was agreed that:

Forasmuch as in the time of this great contagion and sickness diverse and sundry poor persons visited with the same sickness are in so great poverty as they are not able of themselves to relieve their necessity; this day therefore Mr Mayor and Aldermen here present do agree that every Aldermen shall give presently toward the relief of the same visited and sick persons 20 shillings which shall be put into a chest remaining in this chamber for that only purpose. And that every Aldermen shall name and appoint one sufficient person in his several ward to be distributor of the same contribution, which shall in this Court from time to time receive such sums as shall be delivered him in this Court, and then faithfully truly and charitably distribute and give the same money to such persons as be visited with sickness within their several wards whereof they are appointed distributors. And the Sheriffs that now be, and each on that has been Sheriff, to pay 13s 4d. And the payment of the commons to be divided into three parts, viz the best sort to pay 10 shillings, the second sort 5 shillings, and the third sort 2s 6d, which common shall be assessed by the discretion of the Aldermen of their wards. And likewise such widows as shall be thought meet by the Aldermen to be assessed thereto by the Aldermen at their discretion. Which said sums to be distributed as is abovesaid and this to continue for one month.

The same meeting introduced the principles of isolation and lockdown for the first time, and indicated the means by which they were to be enforced:

It is agreed by Mr Mayor and his brethren that every person whose house is visited with sickness of the plague and where any person has or does die thereof do not go abroad by the space of six weeks. And that the poor whose houses are or shall be visited shall be provided for in such manner as they shall have no just cause to go abroad at all, in pain that every offender shall be said in the stocks by the constable or constables of every ward.

It was not until the following year that more detailed rules were introduced:

Mayor's Court Saturday 19 March 1580: Mr Mayor and his brethren considering the continuance of the sickness of the plague in this city are agreed that a certain writing shall be published in the parish churches of this city in the name of Mr Mayor. The contents of which writing are perused and agreed unto by the Aldermen of this house Aldermen two Court days now last passed. And the said Aldermen with one consent do promise to save harmless Mr Mayor in and for the publishing and execution of the same and of every article or clause therein contained the tenor of which writing hereafter ensueth viz:

By the Mayor

For avoiding the increase and spreading of the infection of the plague within this city such as by good policies may be done, it is commanded by Mr Mayor and his brethren that none of any houses so infected within this city or suburbs of the same within one month last passed or which should hereafter be infected shall come abroad into any street, market or shop or open place of resort within the city or the liberties or suburbs of the same at any time hereafter until the plague be ceased in the same house by the space of 20 days at the least, but that every of them shall have and bear in his or their hand or hands openly one white small wand of the length of two foot without hiding or covering the same close from sight. And such as carry wands not to come to the Guildhall nor at any common lectures or sermons upon pain of every such offender sent by any alderman or constable or being convicted before any alderman, to be set in the stocks by any alderman or constable or constables from the time of his apprehension and convicting until eight of the clock in the afternoon of the same day. And then from time to time to be punished as often as any offence is in that manner committed, or else to pay for every time offending five shillings to the use of the poor.

Also that the clerk or sexton of every parish or one of them do with all convenient speed set upon the doors of every house so visited with sickness of the plague one paper with these words written therein:

LORD HAVE MERCY UPON US

And to see that the same be not pulled down until the plague be ceased in the same house by the space of one month. And if it be pulled down then to cause another like bill to be set in the same place by the clerk or sexton of every parish where such visited house is, the same clerk or sexton taking for doing thereof two pence for every time to be paid by the churchwardens of every parish on pain to lose ten shillings. And every person pulling down or causing to be pulled down any such paper to lose ten shillings or to be otherwise to be punished at the discretion of the magistrates of this city.

Also that no person within this city the liberties or suburbs of the same, now having or that shall have any plague sore upon them shall come abroad into any street market shop or open place of resort aforesaid until 20 days after the said sore be fully whole upon pain of everyone so offending to be set in the stocks by Mr Mayor or any alderman or constables commanding of this city.

Also that no dweller in this city sell any household stuff whereby any peril of infection may grow or arise before the first day of the month of May now next ensuing and then only by and at the discretion of Mr Mayor and his brethren.

The doors and windows of the houses would be boarded up so that nobody could get in or out. This would happen as long as there was plague in the house and, according to these regulations, for one month after the last plague victim in the house had recovered or died, so that the period of incarceration might be two months or even more. This appears to have been the first time such rules were introduced in the city: in later years, Orders—no doubt anxious to prevent a second spike—extended the quarantine period from a month to five or even six weeks from the date of the last infection or death within the household.

Parish registers have a lot to tell us about the 1579 outbreak. They survive for this year for 25 out of the 34 parishes that made up the city of Norwich. On examination, the registers for one parish appear to be incomplete—the register for St George Tombland records no burials at all for twenty months between 11 June 1579 and 8 March 1581. Some registers note the arrival of the plague, but not necessarily at the same time. The St Benedict's register, before an entry for 2 May 1579, says 'A fatal plague swept the city'. The register for Saints Simon and Jude has a note in August 1579: 'The Greate Plage'.

The 24 parishes for which registers survive record a total of 1,926 burials for the calendar year of 1579. The numbers vary from over 200 in two parishes (248 in St Stephen, 243 in St Peter Mancroft) down to less than two dozen in another two (20 in St Edmund, just 17 in Saints Simon and Jude). These are total burials for the year: in no parish is any attempt made by the parish clerk to distinguish plague burials from other burials. Of course, the parishes varied enormously in terms of size, both in area and in population, so it is difficult to calculate which were worst hit in the terms of proportion of parishioners killed. There was no head counting of numbers in each city parish before the 'census' made in 1693, which is included in Appendix Four. It seems probable that, although the *numbers* in 1693 were a good deal higher than they would have been a century earlier, perhaps roughly double, the *proportion* of people living in each parish in the city may well have been much the same. In 1693, St Peter Mancroft and St Stephen were indeed the two most populous parishes in the city (with over 1750 inhabitants each), while St Edmund and Saints Simon and Jude were among the smallest parishes (with less than 500 inhabitants each).

In order to get some sense of which parishes were worst hit, I have adopted another approach: I have looked at the average number of yearly burials in each parish in the five 'normal' years before the plague, 1574-1578. By seeing how great the leap is for burials in the single year 1579, one can get an impression of how badly each parish was affected. In the least affected parishes, there were four or five times as many burials in 1579 as the average in the previous years. In the worst affected parishes, there were twenty or more times as many. One parish stands out: in St Lawrence, where the rate was 45 times as many. This is because this parish register records all the burials of Strangers, who make up almost half the burials: no other parish does this. If the Strangers are discounted, St Lawrence remains one of the worst hit parishes, with more than twenty times the number of burials than in a normal year. Similar rates are found in St Peter Southgate, St Peter Parmentergate and St James Pockthorpe, with All Saints and St Stephen not far behind. In contrast, parishes where the number of burials in 1579 is 'only' about five times that of a normal year include St Benedict, St John Timberhill, St Martin at Palace, St Michael at Plea, Saints Simon and Jude and St Saviour. To put it crudely, an individual was four times as likely to die of plague in 1579 in the former group of parishes than in the latter.

It is natural to assume that plague would have most effect in the poorer parts of Norwich: obviously it would be harder to socially distance in a crowded tenement where a whole family might live in a single room than in a large merchant's house, such as Stranger's Hall, to take a surviving example (now an excellent museum). Some idea of where the poor were concentrated in the city can be seen in the Norwich census of the poor of 1570: the wards with the highest percentage of the city's poor were Ber Street, West Wymer and Fyebridge. These do include most of the parishes mentioned above as being worst affected by plague, but it is a mistake to be too simplistic: all wards and all parishes will have contained some relatively prosperous house fronting the main streets, with poor people concentrated in the tenements and yards behind in conditions of poverty almost inconceivable today.

The 1570 census gives details of the lives of the poor in the city. Many were aged and will have died by 1579, but a few can be identified as likely plague victims for example:

**Margaret Togg** of St Martin at Palace. In 1570, she was 30 years old, lame, and spun wool—she is described as 'very poor'. Margaret was buried at St Martin at Palace on 13 September 1579.

**William Dale** of St Peter Mancroft. In 1570, he was 38, an out-of-work glazier, with a wife and three children. He was buried at St Peter Mancroft on 29 August 1579.

**Thomas and Margaret Sawer** of St Gregory. In 1570, Thomas was 30, a cordwainer; his wife Margaret was 40 and earned money from knitting. They had at least one child aged two years. Margaret Sawer, 'wife of Thomas Sawer', was buried in St Gregory's on 26 April 1579. Two later burials—Thomas 'son of Thomas' on 11 August and John Sawer on the following day—are probably their children.

At St Peter Mancroft, there was an average of seventeen burials a year between 1570 and 1578: there were 243 burials in the one year of 1579 alone. St Stephen has similar figures: the average number of burials in the nine years before 1579 is sixteen; in 1579 there are 248 burials. All the ten parishes show a great increase in the number of burials but the increase in these two parishes is the most dramatic. In St Benedict and St Martin at Palace, two much smaller parishes, the average numbers of burials was about six a year in the nine years before 1579: the number in 1579 is 41 and 40 respectively.

*The churchyard of St Peter Mancroft.*

The great peak of the plague was in July or August in most parishes. The 1579 burials at St Peter Mancroft include 106 in August alone. In the tiny parish of Saints Simon and Jude there were only seventeen burials in 1579; however this is still a great increase on the average of only three a year in the previous nine years. The seventeen 1579 burials at Simon and Jude include eight in August and seven in September.

The registers allow us to create the effect of the plague on individual families. To take just four examples from different parishes:

St Lawrence parish:

| | |
|---|---|
| 3 August | Sarah, daughter of Thomas Alcock |
| 11 August | Thomas, son of Thomas Alcock |
| 12 August | Abraham, son of Thomas Alcock |

| 14 August | Thomas Alcock |
|---|---|
| 22 August | Anthony Alcock |
| 23 August | Susan Alcock |

St Peter Mancroft parish:

| 3 July, | Ledea, sister of Francis Phips |
|---|---|
| Same day | Frances, daughter of Francis and Elizabeth Phips |
| 4 July | Nicholas, son of Francis and Elizabeth Phips |
| Same day | Ann, daughter of Francis and Elizabeth Phips |
| 5 July | Francis, Phips senior |
| 6 July | Charles, son of Francis and Elizabeth Phips |
| Same day | Elizabeth Phips. |

St Stephen parish:

| 6 September | Elizabeth, daughter of Edward Barber |
|---|---|
| Same day | Henry, son of Edward Barber |
| 9 September | James, son of Edward Barber |
| 19 September | Anthony, son of Edward Barber |
| 21 September | Robert Reade and Margaret Waterbapp, apprentices to Edward Barber. |

Apprentices lived in their master's house and presumably were locked in with the rest of the family when plague broke out in the house. Deaths of apprentices are quite common in the (relatively few) parish registers of the sixteenth century that record occupations: there are more than a dozen others in St Stephen's in the second half of 1579, for example. Margaret is the only girl among them, presumably reflecting the fact that far fewer girls were apprentices rather than any gender bias among plague victims. Girls can be found in domestic service, as in the next example:

*The churchyard at St Stephen's where many plague victims were buried.*

St Gregory parish:

| 28 July | unnamed daughter of the Kiddles |
|---|---|
| 10 August | Eizabeth, the Kiddle family's maid |
| 16 August | John Kiddle |
| 18 August | Elizabeth Kiddle. |

Other examples of servants or apprentices dying together with family members appear in St Gregory's parish. Thomas Hyssham lost his servant, James Hoyle and his son Christopher Hyssham on the same day, 24 June: just five days later, Thomas Hyssham himself was buried. Thomas Allen lost one servant, Elizabeth Aynsworth, on 5 July and another, Tobie Goodey, two days later. It was six months before his own daughter, Elizabeth Allen, died; buried on 18 January 1580: she was two years and nine months old.

It is sometimes possible to reconstruct a family, especially if they remained within one parish for a long time. I take just two examples, both from St Peter Mancroft. On 14 November 1568, Henry Dudgin married Ozee Paworthe in the church (the name Ozee is unusual but not unique as we shall see). Daughter Faith was baptised there on 7 October 1576, son Henry on 28 May 1579. Then, later in 1579, came tragedy, with the following burials:

| 24 August | Margery Dudgin |
| 5 September | Henry Dudgin |
| 6 September | Faith Dudgin |
| 8 September | Henry Dudgyn [sic]. |

No more information is given in the burial register, but from the evidence of the baptism register Faith was just under three years old, and son Henry (whichever one he is) just on three months. It is not clear whether 'Margery' is a mishearing for Ozee, or whether she is an otherwise unidentified family member. Another family in the parish with the forename Ozee was that of Robert and Jane Hall. Robert was a saddler by profession, living in St Peter Mancroft parish; his daughter Ozee was baptised there on 15 September 1598. They too suffered in the epidemic of the summer of 1603. Ozee was buried on 11 August, a month before her fifth birthday. Robert soon followed his daughter to the grave: he was buried on 23 August.

Several burial registers give no information beyond the name and the date of burial, so it is not always possible to attempt family reconstitution. An unusual name helps: the following five people named in the St Peter Mancroft burial register for 1579 must surely be members of the same family, although the exact relationship is not always clear:

| 31 July | Joane Tenthonica |
| 8 August | Tenthonica, 'his child' |
| Same day | John Tenthonica |
| 12 August | Mary Thenthonica |
| 24 September | Thomas 'ye son of Tentonica'. |

As these examples show, it was very common for the plague to spread through members of a household over a period of three weeks or so, with the household lockdown being extended each time there was another victim. The Phips family's tragedy, losing seven members within four days, is very unusual. Of course, there is no way of being certain that all the deaths were from plague. It should be noted that causes of death are never given in these parish registers: even at the height of the epidemic there must obviously have been some people dying of other causes.

It is often said in Norwich that the plague was brought to the city by the entourage of Queen Elizabeth when she visited the city in August 1578. Blomefield, writing in about 1740, says:

'Queen Elizabeth visits Norwich' (NRO, SO 26/211).

'the Traines of her Majesty's carriage being many of them infected, left the Plague behind them, which afterwards so increased and continued as it raged a whole year and three quarters after', in which time 2335 English and 2482 Alyen Strangers died, from August 20 1578 to February 19 1579, among which were ten aldermen.

Blomefield states his quotation in the above is from something he calls 'the Norwich Roll'. This is clearly not the so-called Mayor's Book (which in any case is not a roll) recording events in the city. This book says nothing about plague in 1578, and simply says of the year 1579: 'this year there deceased in the city of all diseases 4,841 persons'. Unfortunately it does not make clear exactly what it means by 1579, probably the mayoral year beginning June 1579 and running to June 1580.

Blomefield uses the Norwich Roll as a source for his information in the events of the reign of Edward VI in six footnotes, and five more in his chapter on the reign of Elizabeth: it is also referred to twice in the text of his chapter about Norwich in Elizabeth's reign. Reading these, it is clear that the writer of the Roll had a great deal of personal knowledge about Kett's Rebellion of 1549, of which he says at one point that he was an eye-witness, and was then above 22 years of age. He was clearly someone of importance in Norwich: according to another of Blomefield's footnotes, the writer of the Roll records that he was present in the Guildhall chamber in Easter Week 'with the Mayor and others' in 1580, when an earthquake was felt. Unfortunately, the Roll itself has long disappeared. When William Henry Russell compiled his great work on Kett's Rebellion (published in 1859), he says of it 'now, unfortunately no longer in existence' (he cites some extracts from it he read in a pamphlet written by W Chipperfield in about 1800).

Because it no longer exists, we do not know the context of the quoted words, or whether the rest of the sentence is derived from the Roll or is Blomefield's own. It is **definitely wrong** on one point, the deaths of the ten aldermen: this was twenty years earlier, (and is mentioned in the right place in Blomefield. Armstrong also states that the aldermen died in 1579 but, as often, he is just copying Blomefield). Certainly 1578 was a plague year in London, but is he **wrong** in implying that the plague in Norwich began on 20 August 1578, which would coincide with Elizabeth's visit from 16 to 22 August?

The evidence of the majority of the city's parish registers is that the plague did not break out in August 1578, but in the summer of 1579. I have looked at a sample ten of these. The average number of burials in these ten in the early 1570s (1573-1577) was 82 a year. In 1578 there were 95 burials, only a little above the average. In 1579, there were no less than 890 burials in these ten churches. In the following year, 1580, there were 120 burials, falling in the next couple of years to the pre-plague average. This seems to make it clear that the plague did not break out on a large scale in 1578 but in 1579, with a small second spike, to use contemporary terminology, in 1580.

The royal visit was almost ten months before the note of the plague in the St Benedict's register, so that if it was brought by the royal visitors, it must have lain dormant for a long time. And, of course, there were always traders and travellers of all kinds moving into a city like Norwich from places like Yarmouth or London. To take just one example, the 1579 burials at St Gregory include two 'wanderers whose names are unknown' on 18 and 19 July. People like these are just as likely to have been the carriers of the disease.

However, if we look at the records of the parish church of St Martin at Palace a different picture emerges. As the name suggests, this church stands just outside the gates of the Bishop's Palace, which is where Queen Elizabeth stayed when she was in Norwich in August 1578. This parish does seem to show a 'spike' in the number of burials in the aftermath of the Queen's visit, although the numbers are so small it is difficult to be certain what was going on. The parish was very small: there were only three burials in the year 1577 and just four in the first months of 1578. The number of burials then leaps up to seven in the month of September, with six more burials in the following three months.

Three of the first four burials come from one family. The names are:

| | |
|---|---|
| 6 September | Alice Topps |
| 8 September | Alex, son of Thomas Betts |
| 11 September | Alice, daughter of Thomas Betts |
| 15 September | Robert, son of Thomas Betts. |

It is *possible* that these people were the first victims of the outbreak of plague, which, after a period of dormancy in winter, was to emerge in 1579 and devastate the city. Somebody certainly thought that this was what happened: by the heading for the entries for 1578, in what looks like a contemporary hand, has been added (in Latin): PLAGUE PERVADES THE TOWN. Perhaps Blomefield was right and it was the Queen and her followers who brought the plague with them to Norwich, with disastrous results for the city.

## Key Workers

This phrase is applied today to those marvellous health workers who look after the sick in hospitals, surgeries and care homes, and also to those who keep life going by supplying food, clearing rubbish, running essential public transport and similar work. It is never used in earlier times, but there were four groups of people appointed by the city during a time of plague who surely deserve the title. These were:

**Searchers**: to examine the body of every person who died and decide whether the death was caused by plague. This was a simple external examination of the body, made by a person with no medical qualifications. There is no description in the Norwich documents of what was to be looked for. However, the Privy Council orders of 1666 refer to the 'usual signs of the Plague, viz Swellings or Risings under the Ears or Arm-pits, or upon the groynes [groin]; Blains [blisters], Carbuncles or little Spots, either on the Breast or back, commonly called Tokens'. Most people never saw a doctor (few and expensive), so this was the only 'medical' judgement made about whether anyone had the plague. It was not very satisfactory, as some forms of plague (septicaemic) did not produce spots, whereas some diseases other than plague did produce spots. Nevertheless, this remained the key judgement on which the figures were based and upon which the authorities made their decisions. At one point the chancellor of the diocese of Norwich criticised the value of these 'old blind women, whose judgements is as dim as their eyes, and will censure it to be the plague, if a body dies spotted, either with the pox or spotted fever'. He recommended that an elderly Swiss doctor living in the city do the work instead, but the authorities did not follow his advice, and women continued to be appointed searchers if there was plague in the city.[2]

**Bearers**: to carry the body to its place of burial. They are sometimes referred to as 'bearers and buriers'. It must have been very hard to find people desperate enough to take on this work, and perhaps some form of pressure was applied. In 1632, the Mayor's Court decided that a My Hill of St Paul's parish should be a burier 'if he can be persuaded thereunto'.

It is perhaps surprising that there is only one known record of a Norwich bearer failing in the performance of his duties: one man, appointed a bearer by the city, stole goods from a house from which he was removing a dead body (perhaps regarded as an especially low act, like stealing from houses after air raids in the Second World War). He then compounded his crime by running away to Yarmouth with a 'lewd woman', eventually winding up in Colchester.

**Keepers**: to provide food and drink to the infected, when confined to their own house. If the people in the house could afford it, they were expected to pay for this, but if the family were too poor, then the food and drink was supplied free of charge at the city's expense. The idea of an elderly and infirm person employing a keeper to look after them is not uncommon—I have seen references to 'keepers' of old people acting as witnesses in testamentary disputes, for example. The plague-time keepers were different: they were appointed by the city authorities and paid for by them, and were for any plague-struck family, not just the infirm. After the pest-house was established, keepers were also appointed to supply food and drink to its inhabitants.

**Watchmen**: to keep guard at the city gates in time of plague (and, later, near the pest-house), to make sure that no unauthorised person came in or went out. Sometimes a watchman was appointed to guard an individual home, as at Mr Harwyn's house in 1625 and Mr Howse's house in 1631: both incidents are discussed later. If this were done for every infected house, a whole army of watchmen would be needed: perhaps it was done when the inhabitant was thought to be someone especially likely to disobey—as Mr Howse clearly was!

These people had to be paid for out of the city treasury, adding enormously to the expense of an outbreak of plague, but also providing at least some employment for the very poor, and therefore a little movement of cash during a time of economic crisis. The few references indicate bearers and keepers being paid four shillings a week, and there is a reference to a watchman being paid five shillings a week. When Margaret Hill was appointed a searcher, her pay was fixed at 4s 6d a week plus two pence for each body she searched, a small reward for such gruesome work.

There are occasional references to the appointment of all these types of people within the Mayor's Court documents, but many more must have existed, probably appointed by the individual aldermen, with no formal record surviving. Judging from the known examples, searchers and keepers were female, bearers and watchmen male.

Various figures survive among the city records for the number of deaths in the 1579 outbreak: they are inconsistent partly because they cover different timespans. The weekly figures given to the Mayor's Court between 21 June 1579 and 27 February 1580 come to a total of 4,588. Blomefield says that between 20 August 1578 and 19 February 1579 a total of 4,817 people died: he must surely mean August 1578 to February 1580, as most of the deaths came in the summer of 1579. The Mayor's Book counts the number of dead in the mayoral year of June 1579 to June 1580: it gives a total of 4,841 for this period. All these figures are for the total number of burials in the city: they do not distinguish those who died from plague from the other burials. Assuming the usual number of non-plague burials, in all perhaps a quarter of the population died from plague totalling 4,200–4,300.

## The Strangers

The word 'Stranger' can refer to anyone who is not legally a member of the community. In Norwich, it is very commonly used to mean a specific group of people—Dutch and French speaking refugees from the Spanish Netherlands who fled from religious persecution in their own country. They came into the city after 1566, and by 1576 are thought to have made up between a quarter and a third of the population of the city. They were thus present in Norwich during the great plague years of 1579 and 1603, and they appear to have been especially badly hit by the outbreaks.

From 31 October onwards, the weekly mortality returns given to the Mayor's Court differentiate the English-born from the Strangers. This was after the plague had passed its peak. Omitting one week in December when the figures are not complete, the results are stunning: no less than 74% of burials were of Strangers. If this proportion was the same throughout the plague period of 21 June 1579 to 27 February 1580, then 3,395 of the burials would be of Strangers. However, this does seem far too high, so perhaps for some reason there were more Stranger deaths in the period after 31 October than before. Blomefield's figures suggest that 51% of the burials in his, slightly different, time period were Strangers (2482 aliens out of 4817 burials). All the figures make clear that the Strangers died of the plague at an even greater rate than the English: they made up 'only' one third of the population, but at least half the deaths came from among their ranks.

The Strangers had their own places of worship, but no burial grounds: their dead were buried in the churchyard of the local parish church. The work I have done on the parish registers for 1579 shows that very many of these burials are simply not recorded.

A number of burial registers do record the names of some of the many strangers whose deaths are recorded in the figures before the Mayor's Court: these appear to be parishes where there were not many Strangers. The 1579 burials at St Michael at Plea, for example, include several Dutchmen: such as the family of William Bartringham, 'the painter, Dutchman': daughter Judith on 7 Aug, son David on 26 Aug, William himself on 30 Aug, Esther, another daughter, on 24 September.

Two other people described as Dutchmen, were also buried at St Michael at Plea during the plague months. Peter Wallingham, 'Dutchman' was buried in September while another Dutchman, 'Father Israel, the Dutch preacher', was buried on 11 December (his title might suggest he was an important figure in the incomer community, but I have seen no mention of him in any other record). In contrast, Nicholas van Warwyken, buried on 1 November, is not recorded as being Dutch despite his name: if the parish clerk is being scrupulously accurate, Warwyken had presumably taken steps to become a denizen, so that he was no longer regarded as an 'alien'. However, it could well simply be inconsistent recording.

The burial registers of St Stephen's also record the names of Strangers buried in 1579. The word used in the register is 'Extraneus'. Most of the deceased came from just two families. On 20 July, a person named as Purskyre Dyrkyns, Stranger, was buried. There is no indication of the sex of this person, but on 22 July Syrkyn, wife of Purskyre Dyrkyns, was buried, so this was clearly a family of incomers living in the parish. After a gap of just on a month, more of the family are buried: Agnes and Susanna Dyrkyns on 21 August, Abraham Dyrkyns on the following day. If, as seems likely, these were the children of Purskyre and Syrkyn, they had presumably been looked after by other members of the Stranger community after their parents' deaths.

Another family of Strangers within the parish of St Stephen's suffered many deaths in that terrible summer of 1579. A total of seven burials are recorded over a period of less than a month:

| | |
|---|---|
| 18 July | Agnes Lynnes wife of John Lynnes Stranger. This has been amended to read: Agnes wife of Lynnes de Hussura, Stranger |
| 22 July | Agnes Lynnes daughter of John Lynnes, Stranger. This has been amended to read Agnes Lynnes daughter of Lynnes de Hussura, Stranger |
| 23 July | Judith Lynnes, daughter of John Lynnes de Hussura, Stranger |
| 31 July | Lynnes de Hussura, Stranger |
| 12 August | John Lynnes de Hussura, Stranger |
| 13 August | Sara Lynnes de Hussura, Stranger. |

I do not know what the 'de Hussura' signifies and, in view of the amendments, it appears the parish clerk was not certain either. It could be part of the surname, or a place of origin: if the latter, it would be the only example of this being given in any burial register I have seen. In any case, it brings home the tragedy of the times, with husband, wife and (probably) four children dying.

A third incomer family suffering fatalities in the parish was the Cattore family:

| | |
|---|---|
| 20 October | Maria de Cattore |
| 26 October | Jacob de Cattore |
| 3 November | Margareta de Cattore. |

Even such a well-ordered register occasionally fails to provide full information:

| | |
|---|---|
| 3 December | Johannes, Extraneus. |

It will be noted from these last entries that the forenames were expressed in Latin form, so that Jacob de Cattore could have been called 'Jacob', but equally could have been 'James'. This might also suggest that the 'de Hussura' is a Latin phrase, but I have not been able to identify it.

The burial register for the neighbouring parish of St Peter Mancroft for 1579 is very different. Words like 'Extraneus', 'Dutch', 'Walloon' never occur and nor are there any obviously foreign-sounding names. On 2 October, the burial is recorded of 'one John a stranger', but I imagine that he is a stranger in the sense that he is unknown, rather than a member of the immigrant communities in the city.

In some other parishes, where there were many more Strangers, little or no effort was made to record the names. This is clearly seen in St Lawrence, a parish known from other sources to have had many immigrants. It is the only parish where the number of incomer burials almost matches that of 'natives', but without the individual names, so that you get entries like 'Sarah daughter of Thomas Alcock was buried the tenth day of August and 3 Dutch children the same day'. In the three peak plague months of 1579, the burials recorded in St Lawrence were:

| | |
|---|---|
| July | 15 English, 11 incomers |
| August | 29 English, 27 incomers |
| September | 16 English, 13 incomers. |

I have used the word 'incomers' but this is not used in the register itself. Those buried in July and the first half of August are all described as Dutch, those in the second half of August and in September are usually called 'Stranger', but the word 'Dutch' is occasionally used. For example, 'one Dutch bodie' was buried 19 September, but 'Two strangers' were buried on 21 September. The entries are all in the same hand, so it is not clear what distinction the parish clerk was making: perhaps he used the word 'Stranger' if he did not know (and did not care?) whether the body was that of a Dutch person or a Walloon?

Another parish known to house a high proportion of immigrants was St James Pockthorpe. The burials of (unnamed) incomers are recorded here too:

| July | 17 English, 6 incomers |
| August | 37 English, 7 incomers |
| September | 24 English, 8 incomers |
| October | 9 English, 8 incomers |
| November | 5 English, 4 incomers. |

The percentage of incomer burials in the peak months is much lower than that of St Lawrence, and the community may have been of a different character. Twenty-five of the incomers buried are described as 'French', seven as 'Dutch', just two as 'Strangers'. French means French speakers, that is, members of the Walloon congregation: perhaps they were concentrated in this parish while St Lawrence was a centre of the Dutch speaking community?

The number of deaths had an obvious impact upon the economy of the city. Not only were there many extra expenses during time of plague, but income fell as well. I quote two examples from the Stranger community in the city.

- The number of incomers paying subsidy (tax) dropped by a third, from 1,532 in 1576 to 1,026 in 1581.

- Profits from the Dyer's Hall collapsed. This, used exclusively, by the Strangers, brought the city an income of about £2 in a normal year. In Midsummer 1579, just 14s.6d was received. There was worse to come, the city accountant noting 'this account the time of sickness for want of following ceased and nothing collected for a year and a half'.

The people of Norwich might have been grateful to the Strangers for at least one thing: brandy. Known as aqua vitae, it was thought to be a preventive against plague and, in Norwich, its sale was especially associated with the Dutch immigrants.[3]

The plague in Norwich in 1579 is said to have been one of the three worst outbreaks in provincial England, alongside those at Newcastle in 1636 and Colchester in 1666. It is difficult to imagine how devastating these attacks were—and amazing to think how quickly a town recovered as eager newcomers flooded in from the country to replace the dead.

Great Yarmouth also suffered greatly from plague in 1579. A Latin note in the borough court roll says that the outbreak lasted from April to October and that it affected especially boys and the poor ('pueres et pauperes', perhaps the writer enjoyed the alliteration). According to the note 2,000 souls 'and more' perished, and it would have been worse, but for the liberality of the town and its two bailiffs, Benedict Cubitt and John Couldham.[4]

## 1580-1602

There was a further outbreak Norwich in 1583: Blomefield says that between 20 and 25 people died each week, with a total of between 800 and 900. Once again, it was the 'Strangers' who were worst affected. This outbreak may have been localized. Only one of the sample of ten parishes I have examined shows a great increase in burials: in St Gregory's there were 39 burials in the year, compared with an average in single figures for the other years in the early 1580s. There was a sudden spike in St James Pockthorpe in the following year, 1584: the number of burials shot up to 62 in the year, compared with an average of about a dozen each year. They include four 'French' and ten 'Dutch' buried in October to December 1584: again, their names are not given. In the same year there were 36 burials, five times the average in previous years, in St Giles. The 'extra' burials were in summer, a characteristic of plague (three in August, fifteen in September, eight in October). The burials included that of 'James in the sick house' on 18 September, perhaps an example of a plague death in an institution—but, once again, no causes of death are given in the register.

In 1585, it was St Michael Coslany that suffered a spike but on a much smaller scale: after just three burials between April and June, the number of burials jumped to fifteen in the month of August, and a further nine in September. Again, it is not certain that plague was the cause of this very local spike.

Creighton, writing in 1894, says that there was a further outbreak in 1588, but gives no further details. Perhaps he is thinking of the outbreak in the spring of 1590, when 672 people died of plague in the city in just four months. Schools were closed to prevent the spread of infection. I have not seen any order to this effect, but on 5 September 1590, Dutchman Furmyn Vanwater was charged by the Mayor's Court with keeping a school during a time of plague—he refused to come before the court and was ordered to be put in the stocks. He was told to appear before the court the following week with the minister of the Dutch congregation, but there is no record that he did so. Of course, such an order would not have caused the disruption that similar orders did in 2020: only a small number of the children in the city in 1590 would have been attending at a school anyway.

There were close trading links between Yarmouth, at the mouth of the Yare, and Norwich, just twenty miles upriver. This was thought to be a route frequently taken by plague, so that on several occasions it was ordered that goods taken upriver had to be laid out on the ground to disperse any infection clinging to them, before being brought into Norwich. Yarmouth authorities naturally laid down orders for their own borough, similar to those made by the Norwich aldermen. The 1590 orders of the Yarmouth Assembly provide an exceptionally clear summary of what was expected:

April 28, 1590. Ordered that for preventing the plague lately begun every alderman shall appoint a woman in every ward to visit the house where any sickness or death may happen and to report to the alderman whether it is the plague or not, and if it should prove to be the plague the alderman shall charge every house to be watched and no person to be admitted in or out unless every person going in shall remain there a month. And that the infected house may be provided for, the watchman shall take notice of their wants and inform the alderman thereof, who shall order that their wants shall be supplied, shall take care that all necessary things are provided, and they that are able to be provided at their own charge, and they who are not by a general collection. And that an assessment be made on the inhabitants for defraying the expenses. And every watchman at the sick house to be allowed 8 pence a day and that the alderman of wards shall every Saturday night deliver to the bailiff a list of those who die in the week and of such houses as are infected. And for avoiding God's judgement on drunkenness so common in this town, and to avoid all meetings which may spread the infection, it is ordered that no inhabitant shall resort to any alehouse to eat or drink except in the company of a stranger and for a special business, under penalty of 6 pence for the first offence, 1 shilling for the second, and 3 days imprisonment for the third; the ordinance to be published by the vintners. That all body clothes etc that shall come out of infected houses shall be carried near the north mill or the old haven to the south to be aired, where stakes shall be set up, on pain of having their bedding etc burnt.

As this suggests, the dangers of the infection being passed on by touching objects formerly touched by infected persons was recognized. When Thomas Corie was writing weekly letters to London in 1666, he was quick to reassure the recipient: '[I] do assure you there is noe danger in the receipt of letters from me for there is no infected houses in the parish I live in'. This was probably St Michael at Plea: Corie's father paid rates on the family property there in 1634.

## THE OUTBREAK OF 1603

In 1603 there was a severe outbreak of plague in London, killing perhaps 30,000 Londoners. It was a terrible year for Norwich as well. The outbreak of 1603-4 was not *quite* as dramatic as that of 1579, but still cost many lives, perhaps killing a quarter of the population of the city. The Mayor's Book records for the year 1603: 'This year from 25 June to 23 June in next year [1604] died in city of all diseases 3538 whereof of the plague 3076'. Plague continued until 15 Sept 'but there died not afterwards above the number of 12 in one week. The assizes were both kept at Thetford'. Blomefield also gives the total number of deaths from plague in Norwich as 3,076, no doubt taking it from the Mayor's Book. He does not mention it, but once

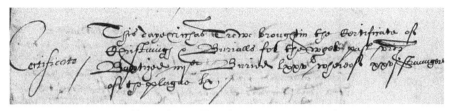

*Weekly certificate of burials, 1603 (NRO, 16a/14).*

again, the Strangers were the worst affected group: historian John Pound estimates that the death rate among this community was twice that of the English. He explains why: 'this high death rate stemmed from the fact that so many worked with cloth and wool (a natural home for fleas) and lived in run-down and rat-infested houses'.[5]

The June dates are not arbitrary but represent the Mayor's year of office. Norfolk assizes were held twice a year, at Easter in Thetford and in July/August in Norwich. The judges came up from London, and the Assize Week was normally a great occasion with dances and other events—'social distancing' would have been impossible so these events were cancelled, like similar public events in 2020.

The outbreak is noteworthy as being the only known occasion when there was discord among the governing body. The Mayor's Court ordered that hangings outside houses be taken down: they were thought to harbour the germs of plague. The Mayor rode about the city to see that this was done. When he came to the house of Alderman Robert Gibson, Gibson taunted him saying '*I would see who dare pull them down*'. However, the Mayor was more than a match for him. Declaring '*That dare I*', he pulled them down himself. Gibson was disenfranchised, but later restored to his place.

As usual, time of plague caused economic problems: Blomefield records that scarcity led to dramatic rises in the price of wheat, rye and barley.

In a small number of parishes, *more* burials are recorded in 1603 than there were in 1579, notably St Giles (114 as compared with 78); St Margaret (122 as compared with 52) and St Peter Parmentergate (97 compared with 85). However, in some parishes badly hit in 1579, the 1603 outbreak saw only about half the number of burials, like St Lawrence (75 as compared with 145) and St Peter Mancroft (118 as compared with 243).

I have looked at the monthly figures for three parishes, St Michael at Plea, St Gregory and St Peter Mancroft. The burials at St Michael at Plea are concentrated in the month of August, whereas those at St Gregory show big increases for three successive months in the summer. The burials at St Peter Mancroft distinguish plague victims for the first time. There were no plague burials at all in 1603 until July when there were four, followed by 29 in August and 37 in September, falling in the autumn but not entirely disappearing: even in February 1604 there were three

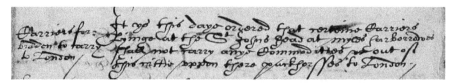

*Mayor's Court order restricting movement of carts to London, 1603 (NRO, 16a/14).*

plague burials. The numbers rose into double figures in the following June, but then fell back: the last plague burials in 1604 were in August.

The 1603 burials at St Gregory show how individual families were affected by the plague: The *Lynne* family, for example lost four members in three weeks: John Lynne, son of John, on 18 July, daughter Rebecca on 26 July, wife Marie on 29 July, John Lynne himself on 3 August. The family was presumably new to the parish as they are not recorded in the baptism registers.

The *Smyth* family also suffered. Marie, wife of John Smyth, on 10 Aug, Rose, daughter of John Smyth, on 21 August, son Thomas 26 Aug, daughter Jane 27 August, Oze Smyth on 2 Oct. Nothing is said of who Oze was in the burial register, but I have searched the baptism register for the parish and found that Osey, the daughter of John Smyth, was baptised on 10 October 1601, so she was another child: she died about a week before her second birthday.

A final example is the *Salter* family. Henry Salter buried two sons, John and Thomas, on 30 Aug, daughter Margaret on 18 Sept. I have looked in the baptism register and these were all the children the family had, so the younger generation was entirely wiped out: the three children were between one and four years old.

North of the river, St Michael Coslany was one of the luckiest parishes in this outbreak of plague; in 1579, there were 81 burials (including twelve Strangers), in 1603 there were just thirteen (none said to be a Stranger). Most of the victims came from just two families in the parish. Plague sometimes struck extremely quickly, as in the household of William Browne:

| | |
|---|---|
| 5 September | Christian Coop, servant of William Browne |
| 8 September | Joane Lowe, daughter of Browne's wife |
| 8 September | William, son of William Browne |
| 14 September | William Browne's wife |

These entries show a chauvinism common in registers of this date: Browne's wife is not even given a name! As it is extremely unusual for anyone to have two forenames at this time, Lowe is most probably a surname: presumably Mrs Browne had earlier been a Mrs Lowe. From this entry, Christian Coop could be either male or female; however, the only person I have found of this name is a female, baptised in Long Stratton in 1575: probably she had followed the common route of leaving her native village to find work in the city.

The name of the wife/mother is again ignored in another family tragedy later in the year in the same parish:

29 November     Joane, daughter of John Parker
16 December     Mary, daughter of John Parker
2 January [1604] George, son of John Parker
6 January        Sara, daughter of John Parker

One family of Dutch immigrants at St Michael at Plea suffered in 1603. James de Hem was buried on 25 Sept 1603, his mother Anna 'and a little infant which had no name', on 5 Oct, and Prudence, the family maid, on 6 December. The de Hem memorial can still be seen in the church, a reminder of the tragedies of four centuries ago in the present-day city. It is not, however, certain that these are plague deaths as the register does not distinguish these from other burials. Anna could simply have died giving birth, all too common in those times, with her new-born child also dying, in which case the deaths of other family members could be just coincidence. The fact that there is a memorial inside the church might indicate it was not a plague burial, as plague victims were not buried *inside* a church, or they could have been buried in the churchyard and the memorial alone placed inside. The memorial, now too faded to read, did indeed say that Anna suffered the fate of Rachel (in the Old Testament, Jacob's wife, who died in childbirth).

Memorial to Anna de Hem in St Michael at Plea church.

In St Peter Mancroft parish, where plague burials *are* indicated, the first burial to be marked in the margin as from plague is that of Francis Alderson, servant to Nathaniel Wolfe, gunsmith. Anderson was buried on 8 July. The word servant is used a lot in this register: probably it usually equates to apprentice, the latter word never occurring in this record. The rest of the family seem to have escaped the outbreak as no Wolfe burials are recorded.

The first family definitely recorded as burials of victims of plague in the parish is the Roding family:

23 July         Elizabeth, the wife of James Roding grocer
31 July         Thomas, the son of James Roding grocer
1 Augus       John, the son of James Roding grocer
4 August      Nicholas, the son of James Roding grocer

16 August            Richard, the son of James Roding grocer

Once again, the pattern of a three-weekly spread of burials within a family shows up.

The St Peter Mancroft register is exceptionally well organised. Not only are plague victims indicated, but occupations are given. Some of the more unusual entries are:

20 August            Edmund Cawston. Innkeeper at the Star.

Deaths of innkeepers are not uncommon, but it is very rare for the name of the inn to be recorded. There were regulations about this: the inn would be closed for the period of quarantine of six weeks, or longer if another inhabitant caught the plague in that time. To indicate this, the inn sign would be taken down, so that people would know it was closed and go elsewhere; despite the obvious dangers of infection, there does not seem ever to have been a general closure of inns in the city, or even in a particular ward.

2 September          Dorothy, daughter of Thomas Hall, schoolmaster
5 September          Anne Leesye, servant to John Lewes, attorney
10 September         William Lewes, brought up by John Lewes, attorney. John
                     Lewes himself and his immediate family do not appear in
                     the burial register so they presumably escaped: it is possible
                     that such a wealthy family had a country estate to which
                     they might retreat in time of plague
12 September         John, son of John Roberts, sexton of this parish
24 September         Anne Dickinse, servant to John Roberts
7 October            Julian, daughter of Henry Baker, musician
13 October           Thomas Lathwell, son in law to William Munning, clerk
10 November          Simon Burrough, goldsmith
23 November          Dorothy, widow of Simon Burrough
26 November          Robert Spurne, servant to Simon Burrough.

At the other end of the social scale, the sad fates of two unfortunate women are recorded:

22 August            Isabell, 'sent from Corter's to a tower where she died'. The
                     possible meaning of this is explained in the section on pest-
                     houses
5 August             Margaret Welch, widow, 'she died in the Castle ditches'.

In St Peter Mancroft, at least, burials of plague victims continued into the winter and into the following year, albeit on a much smaller scale than in the previous year. The figures for plague burials are:

1603, January to June -0; July -4; August -28; September -37; October -15;

November -11; December -5

1604, January -9; February -3; April -7; May -7; June -13; July -5; August to December -0.

Other parishes also show sudden rises of numbers of burials from August 1603. In St Stephen, for example, there were three or four burials a month in the period January to July 1603. The figure rose to thirteen in August, then jumped massively to 44 in September and 43 in October. The rate fell to 25 in November, 24 in December, and 26 in January 1604, still well above the pre-plague figures. Only in February did the number of burials fall back into single figures.

The parish of St Andrew was much smaller, and the effects of the plague much less dramatic. There were just four burials in the church in the whole seven month period of January to July 1603. The figure rose to twelve burials in August falling to six in September and then an average of three a month for the final three months of the year. Of course, the small numbers did not make the situation any less tragic for the families involved, such as the Stanford family:

| | |
|---|---|
| 6 August | Anne, daughter of Nicholas Stanford |
| 16 August | Elizabeth, daughter of Nicholas Stanford |
| 23 August | Nicholas Stanford. |

Once again, the pattern is of plague running through a family in a period of roughly three weeks.

The burial register for All Saints gives a unique insight into details of procedures for burying the dead in the 1603 epidemic. Beside each burial is a figure, presumably the fee for the burial and these vary between nothing and eighteen pence. No indication is given as to how the fee was decided and in a few cases the amount is left blank, as though the clerk himself was unsure. Seventeen people pay nothing, 31 pay four pence or six pence, eight pay between eight and twelve pence, and just two pay eighteen pence.

In six cases, the burial is described as 'chested', which presumably means buried in a coffin. Assuming the clerk is being consistent, this might mean that all the others were buried without coffins. It might be thought that the burials in coffins would incur a higher fee, but this is not the case, as shown here:

| | |
|---|---|
| 18 September | Samuel, son of Peter Bret (12 pence) |
| 19 September | Thomas Goodman (12 pence) |
| 20 September | Henry, the son of Robert Pleasants (10 pence) |
| 27 September | William Scot (6 pence) |
| 8 October | Martha, the daughter of William Fiddes (18 pence) |
| 9 October | Elizabeth, daughter of Thomas Foster (4 pence). |

Martha's burial was unusual in that she is not only said to be 'chested', but also 'buried in church': no other entry that I have seen in this register makes this statement. The costs for this would surely be more, and indeed the fee of eighteen pence is the joint highest in these entries: however, the other person attracting a fee of eighteen pence is not said to have even been 'chested' let alone buried in the church.

It needs to be stressed that the burial register does not distinguish the burials from plague, so a small number of these people will be dying from other causes even in a plague year. It is possible (but pure speculation) that this is indeed the distinction, and that those who died of other causes were buried in coffins, while the much larger number dying from plague were not.

The city had suffered two major epidemics of plague in less than 25 years. However, whereas the outbreak of 1349 seems to have set the city back economically for generations, these Tudor and Stuart outbreaks seem to have had remarkably little effect on city life. The main reason appears to be migration: people coming into the city from the surrounding countryside in search of work and social opportunities. These people were mainly young and single, finding marriage partners in the city and having children there: E A Wrigley has calculated that the average age of people moving to London in Tudor and Stuart times was twenty! Figures given by Wrigley for three Norwich parishes (Peter Mancroft, Stephen and Andrew) show the number of baptisms to be as high, indeed slightly higher, in the 1580s than the pre-plague 1570s. The 1570 Census of the Poor in the city show over half of those listed to be incomers rather than Norwich-born—and the Census does not include any members of the Dutch and Walloon communities (who were responsible for looking after their own poor).[6]

John Patten quotes figures for Colchester that show how quickly a town could recover after an outbreak of plague. The population of the town was about 10,300 in 1662. Heavy plague mortality reduced this to just over 4,000 in 1666. However, within just five years, the population jumped back up to 9,500 and it was soon back to its pre-plague level. There were always incomers ready to fill up the spaces left by outbreaks of plague in a city.[7]

Of course, family life continued even in times of plague, producing many personal tragedies, like that of the Frosdick family in St Julian's. John Frosdick's son, also John, was buried on 14 September. John's (unnamed) wife gave birth just a few days later: their daughter Anne was baptised on 20 September. Sadly, she died on the same day and was buried on 21 September. Another son, Thomas, followed her to the grave just ten days later. These were the unfortunate ones: for those who survived, there must have been much-improved prospects of economic success.

## Strangers

The only parish where burials of immigrants outnumbered those of the English in 1603 was St Margaret. In the 1579 outbreak, there were 52 burials in the parish (for the calendar year), but no burials of Strangers. In 1603, the immigrant community was very badly hit. In this register, once again, the English are given individual names but the immigrants are not. For the four peak plague months of August to November, the numbers of burials are recorded as:

English -53. Immigrant -71

The parish clerk never uses the word immigrant, of course. He has six ways of describing the foreign burials, the distinctions between the categories not always clear to us:

Dutch 'child'    49
Dutch 'maid'     4
Dutch man        9
Dutch woman      3
Dutch 'folks'    5
French 'child'   1

This seems to indicate a large Dutch community within the parish and a very much smaller Walloon one.

In the neighbouring parish of St Lawrence there were almost as many immigrant burials (36) as English (39) during the calendar year 1603. Again, it is the Dutch who predominate: there were 25 Dutch burials, ten of 'Strangers' and just one 'Frenchman'. In St James Pockthorpe parish in the calendar year 1603, there are just five immigrant burials among 74 burials—two Dutch, two French and one 'Stranger'.

St Stephen's parish is one of the few where the immigrants buried are given the dignity of having their names recorded. There are 22 of them out of 176 burials, suggesting a relatively small immigrant community in the parish. They are invariably called 'Stranger', no distinction being made between Dutch and French speakers.

Among the many (87) burials at St Julian's church in the plague year of 1603, are fourteen of people described in the register as 'Strangers', again with no distinction between the two immigrant groups. Family relationships are not always given but the surnames alone show how the plague had a devastating effect on some immigrant families:

16 Sep        Sara Isebrand
23 Oct        Christopher Pomand
25 Oct        Martha Custinople
27 Oct        Susanne Custinople
2 Nov         John Cobbleyon
5 Nov         Pascua Pomand

| 5 Nov | Maria Custinople |
| 20 Nov | Susanne, daughter of Martin Deswarffe |
| 2 Dec | William Leaport |
| 8 Dec | Abraham, son of Martin Deswarffe |
| 15 Dec | John, son of Martin Deswarffe |
| 19 Dec | Sara, daughter of William Leaport |
| 21 Dec | Mary, daughter of William Leaport |
| 30 Dec | Abraham, son of William Leaport. |

Three burials of Strangers were recorded in All Saints in 1603, with the burial fee:

| 18 October | Easther Kettlebutter (18 pence) |
| 19 November | Peter Peane (8 pence) |
| | Jacob de Thye (12 pence). |

The fees are at the higher end of those being charged, but are matched by some of the English burials. None of the Strangers are recorded as having been buried in coffins.

Another source of information is the will. One might expect many more people to make wills in time of plague. In Norwich, this is most noticeable in 1603, among both the Stranger and native community. The preambles of the wills sometimes suggest the presence of plague: about thirty Strangers, aware of the possible imminence of death, made wills. Some were specific about the danger. Peter van Monsey wrote: 'if my wife Peeronel should chance to die of this sickness then is my daughter Easter van Monsy to have all that which we both leave behind us', and Matthew Ployart wrote: 'if it please God to call me out of this world by this sickness'. Andreas Priem also showed his awareness of mortality, writing, 'considering that men are suddenly overtaken by death' and 'if it shall please God to take us all into His kingdom by this sickness'. John Decock wrote his will: 'I have felt myself weakened with the hand of God'.

Another immigrant will was that of Walloon Adrian de la Mee, made 28 September 1603, and proved 9 December 1603. His wife Margaret was also ill, and provisions were made if she were to die before him. His clothes were divided among his sons, while his daughter Anne received 'our best bed whereon my wife and I do lie', with two pillows, two pairs of sheets, the bed coverings and curtains—presumably they would first be thoroughly disinfected if the couple did die of plague in the bed!

## The Cathedral Close

There were 34 parishes within the city of Norwich. Anyone looking at a list of parish registers—for example those made by the Norfolk Record Office for the use of genealogists—might think that the number was 35. However, one parish, although physically in Norwich, was not part of the city, and the aldermen had no authority over it. This was the area of the Cathedral Close, the parish of St Mary in the Marsh. The area was surrounded by walls, with the two massive gates on Tombland (the Erpingham Gate and the Ethelbert Gate). Historian Paul Slack cites Norwich as one of three Cathedral Closes that resisted attempts to involve them in plague rates and watches (the others were Exeter and Salisbury).[8]

The Cathedral authorities were keen to keep out those who might be infected, presumably by closing the gates. This seems to have worked: the burial registers do not survive for St Mary in the Marsh that would cover the 1579 epidemic, but those for 1603 and 1625 show no rise in the (very small) number of burials compared with other years. However, by the time of the 1666 outbreak the character of people living in the Close had probably changed: cathedrals had been abolished under the rule of Parliament but had been restored in 1660. According to the register, 25 people died of plague in the Close in 1666 and were buried in St Mary in the Marsh. A further three burials are described as 'suspected' to be plague victims, an uncertainty I have not seen in any other Norwich burial register. The searchers employed elsewhere in the city would not have looked at the bodies of those dying in the Cathedral Close: perhaps those who buried them, lacking the experience of the professional searchers, were occasionally unwilling to commit themselves. Because the Close was not part of Norwich, these 25 or 28 plague victims do not appear on the official count of those who died of plague in the city.

## Notes

1    Eric S Wood, *Historical Britain* (1995) p.25.

2    Slack, *op. cit.* p.275.

3    The taking of brandy to ward off plague is mentioned in Fernand Braudel, *The Structures of Everyday Life* (1981 edition) pp.241-2. For aqua vitae and the Strangers see Frank Meeres, *The Welcome Stranger* (2018) passim.

4    NRO, Y/C4/273.

5    John Pound, 'Government to 1660' in Carole Rawcliffe and Richard Wilson, eds. *Norwich since 1550* (2004) p.44. Paul Slack had earlier made the same point, indeed in almost the same words: 'most of them [the Strangers] were artisans and labourers, working with cloth and wool (always a ready source of fleas) packed into dilapidated and rat-infested houses'. (Slack, *op. cit.* p.140).

6    E A Wrigley, *Population and History* (1969) pp.114-5. The London figure is quoted by Patten (see next note) and derives from an article by Wrigley in *Past and Present* 37 (1967).

7    John Patten, *English Towns 1500-1600* (1978) p.132.

8    Slack, *op. cit.* p.270.

*St Peter Southgate: people dying in the pest-house were buried here. The churchyard is now a children's playground.*

# Containing the Disease
# 1604 to 1665

AFTER 1603, there was no major outbreak of plague in the city for more than two decades. However, the aldermen remained on the alert. In 1609, although the death rate in that year was not large, the city authorities, according to Blomefield, arranged that "the river was watched 'lest they should bring stuff or infected persons from Yarmouth'". Presumably there was plague in Yarmouth and the Norwich aldermen took this step to try and prevent it entering the city, an objective that appears to have been achieved.

## THE 1625 OUTBREAK

Plague broke out again in Norwich in 1625: Blomefield says that this time it was indeed imported from Yarmouth. The plague is said to have killed 1,431 people in the city between 22 July 1625 and 10 November 1626. The figures for the deaths in 1625 are contained in the weekly reports to the Mayor's court: 861 plague burials are recorded in the year. There were none at all until the week ending 23 July, when there were just two. After another two weeks without plague deaths, the outbreak began to take hold, with 14 in the week ending 13 August, leaping to 67 in the following week and to 77 in the week ending 17 September.

The authorities must have feared the worst, but this turned out to be the worst week in 1625, with rates falling to the low thirties per week in November and to single figures by Christmas. Even during these months of plague, it did not devastate the city as it had in 1579 and 1603. The total number of burials between 23 July and the end of the year was 1,324 so that just under two thirds of the burials were of plague victims: in a bad year, well over 80% of burials would be victims of plague.

The total number of Strangers buried in the same period was 181, or less than 14% of the burials. The record does not say how many of these died from plague, but, even if most of them did, we are clearly in a very different Norwich from 1579 or 1603, when as many Strangers as natives were dying from plague. The number of people forming the Stranger community in the city had become very small as many of the immigrants, and their descendants, had either returned to the Continent or merged into the native population.

This plague was a very patchy outbreak, with relatively large numbers of burials in August, September and October 1625 in the neighbouring parishes of St James Pockthorpe and St Paul, and in St Martin at Palace just over the river. However, other parishes such as Saints Simon and Jude and St Michael at Plea show no more burials than usual during these months.

Again, parish registers often note the beginning and end of an outbreak. The St James Pockthorpe register for August 1625 has the note 'The plague began'; that for March 1626 says 'the plague not yet ceased'. At St Martin at Palace, an entry in August 1625 notes 'The Plague began'.

St Martin at Palace was one of the few parishes that distinguished plague victims from other burials. The first plague victim died in August, and there were total of 28 between that month and November, before the usual winter respite, with no plague burials at all in December 1625 or January 1626. The eight burials in the parish in August 1625 were all from two families: four Paynes and four Oughts. The burials in September include four members of the Bearaway family—Joan on the 6th, Goslyn and Elizabeth on the 13th and John on the following day.

At St Julian, all those being buried between 6 September and 12 December (22 people) are bracketed together as 'PESTE MORTIS'. At St Peter Southgate, three burials from one family are marked with a bold capital '**P**':

2 September       Rebecca Sutton
12 September      Tylney Sutton
20 September      John Sutton.

The '**P**' looks more or less contemporary and the spacing of the burials certainly suggests that the Suttons were victims of plague. As no other entries in the register are marked in this way, either the parish escaped extremely lightly, or the parish clerk was inconsistent in recording plague deaths. However, it is far from certain that the capital letter does indicate plague: several other families in the parish suffered losses in the summer of 1625 that look very like plague, even though they are not given the initial '**P**'. Examples include Susanna and Martha Sharpin, buried on 8 and 20 June, Prudence and Richard Bunting, buried on 30 June and 12 July, and the Burges family: Clement Burges was buried on 2 August, his daughter Hose (? the name is not clear) on 22 October, and his son Thomas four days later. The gaps in the burial dates very much suggest an outbreak of plague in the parish but it is impossible to be certain.

The story of the 1625 plague can also be told from the Mayor's Court Books. Weekly figures were supplied to the court by Ambrose King at first, with John Goodrum taking over from 27 August. Because the outbreak was relatively contained, the aldermen record many more details of how the outbreak was fought, even down to the level of naming individual households. This has given us a much more detailed picture of how the aldermen worked than was possible in the much larger outbreaks of 1579 and 1603.

Orders by the authorities include the following:

4 July: after plague had broken out in Great Yarmouth, boatmen were told not to carry anyone from infected regions to Norwich, a man recently arrived in the city from Yarmouth was ordered to depart. The city was authorized by letters patent to levy a rate to pay for repairing the city walls, cleaning ditches and removing nuisances in the city, to prevent the spreading of the plague that had lately broken out in Yarmouth.[1]

13 July: carriers were commanded not to bring any passengers from London, nor to bring home any wool.

15 July: constables to put two men to watch at every gate of the city (just one for Pockthorpe) every day to keep out all persons coming from London, Yarmouth 'or any other place infected of the plague to come into this city without the consent of the nearest Justice of the Peace or the Alderman of the ward'.

It was also ordered that: 'the Bellman by public proclamation warn all persons within the city to put away their dogs and swine out of the walls, on the pain of being killed' [the animals not their owners!]. A watch was to be kept on infected houses, and a whipping ordered for anyone found begging in the streets.

30 July: decided to end the watch on the gates.

11 August: aldermen could claim money from the city treasurer to help infected families. It was also ordered that the doors of all persons that died of the infection should be nailed up and watched.

25 August: any keepers or watchmen neglecting their duties to be whipped.

1 Sept: The Dutch congregation appointed Peter Heyband to look to the infected poor in their community: he was appointed for 21 weeks. Whenever he went outside, he had to carry a red wand at least a yard and a half long, as did his family.

19 September: 'the Black-Tower on Butter-Hills was made up for a Reception for infected poor, and Tho[mas] Chambers appointed keeper thereof at four shillings a week'. The original appointment was for just one month: presumably a thrifty court hoped that the plague would be over by then: in fact, vouchers show that Chambers was still in post and being paid eight months later. The documents include one bill from him covering three weeks

at the end of April: during this time there were a total of four people in the Tower, three men (Richard Gray, William Bilney and John Brombell) and one woman (Elizabeth Thurston), spending between four and eight days there: conditions can be judged from the payment of four pence to supply straw for two of the men to sleep on.[2]

In the same month, two widows were appointed to search the infected poor, also at four shillings a week, and the same wage was paid to four bearers to collect the dead and take them to the 'burial ground'—was this outside the city or does it simply mean the local parish churchyard?  There must have been a revival of the outbreak the following spring: on 15 March, the six 'plague attendants' (which presumably means the searchers and bearers just mentioned) were ordered to reside in Norman's Hospital (near St Paul's church) and carry red staves one and a half yards in length.

21 September: city gates to be watched and warded. On the same day, each alderman was ordered to find out from the churchwardens and overseers of each parish within his ward how much money had been raised by a rate, who it had been spent on and what money remained in their hands.

On 20 September, Alderman Emes was lent £5 for the infected poor over the water. Four days later, Alderman Spendlove was lent £10 from the funds of the Great Hospital for the infected poor in the wards 'this side of the water'. As this entry shows, the city had to think creatively about raising money during an outbreak of plague. Wealthy citizens might volunteer contributions: in 1625, when Sir John Hobart retreated to the security of the country, he not only offered to pay all the rates and dues he would have paid if he was still resident in the city, he gave ten shillings a week to help. The two sheriffs elected in that year each contributed £10 rather than spending money on the customary celebratory feasts. In November 1625, the city borrowed the large sum of £50 from the wealthy St George's Guild to see them through the crisis.

The Mayor's Court Book did not normally deal in individual families, but the beginning of the 1625 outbreak was an exception, and gives us a uniquely detailed record of the start of an outbreak, and the reactions of the civil powers. On 21 July, the court was told that Mr Harwyn had died that morning of plague. The constables, churchwardens and overseers of his parish, St Margaret's, were ordered to nail boards over the doors of his house and cause it to be watched night and day.

At the court of 11 August, overseers of four parishes brought lists of houses in which people had died, with the numbers of people still living in these houses. They were in four parishes: St Margaret, St Benedict, St Lawrence and St Martin at Oak. The houses involved were:

|  | died | alive | of which sick |
|---|---|---|---|
| ST BENEDICT: |  |  |  |
| Widow Arnold's | 1 | 5 | 2 |
| Edmund Davy's | 1 | 5 | 2 |
| Robert Spooner's | 1 | 3 |  |
| Nathaniel Pinte's | 2 |  |  |
| ST MARGARET: |  |  |  |
| John Webb's | 1 | 5 | 2 |
| Thomas Anderson's | 4 | 4 | 2 |
| Nicholas Spooner's | 1 | 4 | 1 |
| Clement Palmer's | 1 | 3 |  |
| Widow Jaxon's | 1 | 2 |  |
| Widow Doughty's | 1 | 5 | 1 |
| Reade's | 1 | 5 |  |
| Nicholas Brown's | 1 |  | Two persons infected |
| Richard Killingworth's | 1 | 3 |  |
| Harwyn's house | 2 | 4 | 2 |
| Widow Harwyn's house | 3 | 2 |  |
| Whalles' | 1 | 5 |  |
| ST LAWRENCE: |  |  |  |
| William Lowe's | 2 | 1 |  |
| William George's | 1 | 2 |  |
| ST MARTIN AT OAK: |  |  |  |
| Rust's | 2 | 5 | And three in the same yard, two of whom are sick |

The worst affected parish was St Margaret, and by looking at the parish burial registers, it can be seen how the plague affected individual families:

Thomas Anderson lost one daughter, Mary, buried on 30 July followed by a second, Ann, on 10 August. The house was boarded up: the plague was already very active as two more children, Edward and Christopher, were buried on 11 and 12 August. These presumably make up the four mentioned at the Court, Christopher having died on the day of the Court's meeting and being buried on the following day. They were followed by their mother, Mary, just two days later. No more members of the Anderson family died.

Deaths in the Spooner household were more spread out. Four of Nicholas' children died, starting with Mary, buried on 8 August. The house was then boarded up: it was almost three weeks before there were more family burials: William on 27 August, Anne on 9 September, and Nicholas two days later.

In the house of Clement Palmer, his daughter Ellen was buried on 9 August. The house was then boarded up: the only subsequent death was his son Thomas, buried on 20 August.

*The parish church of St Michael at Plea: the parish largely escaped the 1625 outbreak of plague (NRO, N/LM 2/10).*

In the two Harwyn houses, all the deaths came before 11 August: Mary, daughter of William Harwyn was buried on 20 July, followed by William himself on 22 July, and by another daughter, Anne, on 29 July. William is perhaps the only person for whom we have a date of death **and** a date of burial, and this confirms what logic would expect, that burial followed very rapidly: William died on the morning of 21 July and was buried in his local churchyard the following day. Presumably the house was boarded on the same day or very soon after, so that it had already been nailed up for about a week before Anne died. There were no subsequent burials in the family. It is because of William's death in July, that the family is called 'Widow Harwyn's' in the above table drawn up in August.

In the other Harwyn house, the son William died on 5 August, followed by his mother Anne the next day. The house was then boarded up: there were no more family burials.

At the Whall's house, there were two deaths in early August, Mary, the daughter of John Whall, was buried on 8 August, and John's wife Mary on 10 August; the aldermen had presumably not yet heard of her death when they made their list on 11 August. The house was then boarded up: three more children died in quick succession, Margaret, buried on 15 August and John and Rose, both on 19 August. There was then a long period without any deaths and the family must have hoped that the tragedy had reached its peak: however, another daughter, Urseley, was buried on 17 September.

There were other gaps of two or three weeks in these houses in the parish of St Margaret: Arthur Jackson was buried on 10 August, hence the house being correctly described on the following day as 'Widow Jaxon's'. The house was then boarded up: the 'widow', Margaret Jackson herself, was buried on 23 August. The house of Richard Killingworth was boarded up after the death of his son, buried on 6 August: it was not until 25 August that another son, Richard, was buried.

These instances give an impression that children were exceptionally vulnerable. Again, this can be checked from the burial registers. Burials over the three months August to October 1625 comprise 32 described as sons, 29 described as daughters, with 15 males not described, so probably adult, eight females described as wives and another four females with no description, presumably either widows or adult single women. So the number of children buried was twice that of adults, but, of course, there was a far higher proportion of children in the city population four centuries ago than is the case today.

The outbreak continued into 1626, with nineteen plague burials between February and May in St Martin at Palace for example. In March, watchmen were posted near infected houses and those infected forbidden to go out. On 13 May, a man was prosecuted for organizing a bull-baiting in his yard, 'to the eminent peril of the city in this contagious time'. (Entertainments needed a licence from the city magistrates, who often refused even in non-plague periods, perhaps a reflection of their Puritan sympathies. In May 1623 they had declared that public gatherings in general were conducive to the spread of the plague.)

A report to the Privy Council said that the plague had been present throughout the winter of 1625/6 and was now increasing with the warmer weather, 'so that there die very manie weekly, there being 16 of the 32 parishes infected'. The Privy Council ordered the cancellation of the annual Mayor's Feast, the money usually spent on it to be spent instead on relieving the plague-stricken poor and building a pest-house. However, the city sent in a petition and a certificate saying that the outbreak of plague was not *that* serious and that steps were being taken to prevent it spreading: the Privy Council agreed to let the feast go ahead after all.

## THE 1630s

There was a minor outbreak in 1630, described by Blomefield:

In April 1630 the Plague broke out again in St Gregories Parish, one child dying of it, upon which the Court met, and swore a Woman searcher of the infected, nail'd up the Door of the House, and by the Common Crier order'd all Dogs, Cats, tame Doves, Rabbits, and Swine to be put out of the City or killed, and in May the Tower next Brasen-Door was appointed for the Buryers, and for a Prison for such infected Poor as would not be ruled: and the Distemper being much in Cambridge, the Carriers thither were prohibited; six houses were erected on Butter-hills near the great Black Tower there, which was fitted up with them for Pest-Houses, and an Acre of Land about them closed with tall Boards, and Watch-men were set day and night to keep any from going thither, or coming thence, and all that died there were ordered to be buried in the Church-Yard of St Peter at South-Gate; but it pleased God that this great Caution had its desired effect, the distemper not spreading, not above 1 or 2 died in a week.

I have counted the number of burials for each year between 1629 and 1635 in a sample of ten parishes: St Michael at Plea, St Gregory, St James Pockthorpe, St Paul, St Martin at Palace, St Peter Mancroft, St Saviour, St Julian, St Augustine and St Benedict. The mortality is once again very patchy, some parishes being barely affected. At St Martin at Palace, for example, a note before a burial on 10 July 1631 says 'The Plague began'. Despite this there are only five deaths indicated with a 'P', all in July and August 1631, three from one family, the Reimers—Samuel, 10 July; George, 26 July; Phillis, 27 July; William, 3 October— the last not said to be plague. At St Saviour, a note in August 1632 says PESTUS INCIPIT and the total number of burials in 1632 at sixteen is five times the average of the previous three years. However, at St Peter Mancroft the number of burials in 1631 and 1632 is *lower* than that in 1629 or 1630, so that the plague of the early 1630s had no effect at all in this parish.

Details of the 1630 outbreak of plague can be traced in the records of the Mayor's Court. In the three months of August to October, 25 meetings were held. The Mayor (William Browne) attended every one and the two sheriffs were also at almost all of them. Of the 23 other aldermen, seven attended two-thirds of the meetings. Four of them were former mayors, and therefore Justices: Thomas Blosse, Alexander Anguish, Robert Craske and Robert Debney. The three other aldermen attending most meetings were Thomas Shipdham, Robert Hornsey and Thomas Atkin. The remaining aldermen attended much less frequently, often just once or twice in the three months. The City Steward, John Jermy, and the City Recorder, William Denny, might attend but hardly ever did so: each was at just one meeting in the three month period. The city was effectively in the control of ten men: the Mayor, the two sheriffs and the seven aldermen who attended most of the meetings: it was these men who made decisions about isolation and lockdown that decided the economic fate and even the actual lives of their fellow citizens and their families.

On 26 June, two people were reported to have died of the plague in the previous week. Watchmen were appointed to attend the pest-houses on Butter Hills, to keep other people away and restrain those in the house from going out, and also to provide them with provisions and 'reasonable wages'. John Camp was ordered to kill any dogs, hogs, cats and tame doves that he found in the streets 'because of the danger of Contagion'. He was told to bury the corpses.

Unusually the Court met again just two days later, on the Monday. Much of the business was concerned with plague. It was ordered that a watchman be set up at Ber Street and another at South Conesford to watch near the pest-house and make sure no one tried to escape under cover of darkness. A man named Robert Foakes was to watch in

*Norwich city walls and Black Tower: the pest-houses were in this area of the city.*

the daytime, for which he was to be paid four shillings a week: in September, it was ordered that he should actually reside in the Tower. A Mrs Sandcroft was to provide provisions and to carry water to the pesthouse for which she was to be paid seven pence a day. The bearers of the bodies of plague victims were given a bonus of twelve pence a week to provide them beer. Financial arrangements were finalised: the overseers of the parish involved were to pay 2s. 6d. a week to any infected person taken to the pest-house, for which they would be re-imbursed by the 'Treasurer of the Infected'. One particular case was also under consideration: William Hafford who was in self-isolation ('still shut up') was to be paid ten shillings a week by the overseer of his (unnamed) parish.

On 1 July it was decided that if anyone died while in the pesthouse, the corpse was to be buried in St Peter Southgate churchyard. This was the nearest parish church, so minimized the distance the bodies needed to be carried through the streets by the bearers. There is no indication in the parish burial register of any burials from the pest-house: perhaps they were not recorded.

On 3 July it was reported to the court that there had been no deaths from the plague in the previous week. However, the difficulty of diagnosis in some cases was demonstrated at the same court. Agnes Lambert said that she had been employed to search the body of Robert Kettle. She said that she had arrived at his house at 7 pm the previous night: Kettle was already dead. She stayed all night and in the morning put him into his winding sheet: she saw no reason to think he had died from the plague, as there were no 'tokens' on his body. In a similar incident in the same year, two searchers reported that a child did not die of plague because 'there is nothing to be seen, neither spot nor rising.'

The Kettle incident indicates how swiftly events could move. Kettle died on 2 July. He was buried in St Peter Mancroft on the following day, the Court meeting on the same afternoon. No other person named Kettle appears in the burial register for July or August, so if Kettle did indeed have the plague he did not pass it on to his family. On the same day, 3 July, the Court was told by a Robert Dey that two people, Richard Arnold, grocer, and his wife, had been at Kettle's house since Kettle had died  This must have been on the day he died or the following morning, so perhaps they were simply expressing sorrow at a friend's death. Dey was not an alderman, so was probably a marshal, paid by the court to keep an eye on things, but possibly could be simply a citizen doing what he saw as his public duty, informing on those who had broken the rules of isolation. There is no record of the Court taking any action against the Arnolds.

As we have seen, plague brought many expenses to a town, and the authorities might have to beg other towns to help. There was an outbreak of plague in Cambridge at this time: the Court gave £6. 14s. 6d. for their relief, the money being taken there by one of the aldermen, Augustine Skottowe. The city also needed to look at its own financial situation: on 7 July, it was ordered that a rate be made for the infected poor of the city.

Just one person died of the plague in the week ending 10 July, and in the next few days three houses that had been shut up because of infection were opened up: in the case of the Tolls, we are told they had been shut up six weeks since anyone had died there. William Hafford's house had been shut for ten weeks: how relieved they must have been to be told that 'they were now at liberty to go abroad'.

On 21 July, the Dutch were told they could take down their pest house: this had been built on land belonging to alderman Sir Peter Gleane. There were no new plague deaths and, on 14 August, widow Coe and 'goodwife' Banister of St Margaret's, who had been shut up for over seven weeks, were told they could go out, although the officials were still cautious: Robert Howse the younger, one of the parish churchwardens, was instructed to order them not to 'thrust themselves into company' for a time. Ministers were told to hold thanksgiving services in their parish churches on 17 August, while a sermon was given in the Cathedral. On 28 August, the buriers were ordered to be discharged on the following Monday. The Court ordered that the clothes belonging to Chambers' daughter be burnt and that she be given new apparel. Bedding was to be carried into the Tower and there aired. Chambers had been appointed keeper of the pest-house in 1625 and no doubt served in the same position once more: it is not clear if the bedding was that of himself and his family, or of the pesthouse as a whole.

This outbreak of plague was over, and the city was right to be thankful: there had only been three deaths from plague between 26 June and the end of the year.

The next year, Norwich was not so fortunate.

The outbreak of 1631 is first mentioned at the court of 9 April. No plague deaths were reported to the Court but it had plainly returned to the city. Alderman Thomas Shipdham told the court that it had broken out in St Augustine's parish: in one house a man named John Decore had died and other houses had become infected  The court told Shipdham and another alderman, Alexander Anguish, to take charge of the situation. They were instructed to order the nailing or locking of the doors of any houses where infected people were living—and also the houses of anyone who had been in the infected houses, even if they showed no sign of infection. This forced self-isolation of anyone known to have been in contact with the infected was very much the seventeenth century version of the 'track and trace' of the twenty-first century, but, of course, without the 'app'.

It was reported to the court that two houses were affected. In one, three people had died, one three weeks ago, one on Thursday 31 March, one on Sunday 3 April. There were now three people alive in the house—a man, a woman and a child. In the other house, one person had died three days ago and two more on the night before the court: there were now just a woman and two children in the house. However, this was because the children's father, Adrian Latrye, had taken matters into his own hands: he had put another of his children into the house of a widow Levine and himself moved into the house of Joseph Latrye, presumably a relative. This dispersal of possibly-infected persons was of course exactly what the aldermen were desperate to avoid and father and child were ordered back into their own house to face compulsory lock-in.

Incidentally, nothing of this vivid story from the Mayor's Court book could be deduced from the St Augustine's burial register, which records just one burial in the whole of April, Isaac Abbot, the son of Daniel Abbot, baptised 3 April and buried the same day: if he died of plague he was clearly one of its youngest victims. The names Decore and Latrye sound as though they could be members of the Walloon community, which was especially affected, as we shall see, by this particular outbreak, and perhaps therefore not recorded in the local parish burial register.

The now-usual steps were taken. Bearers were re-appointed and a Mrs Newlands appointed to be searcher, and the bearers and the searcher were themselves ordered to be locked in. In tracking the origin of the outbreak in the parish, suspicion seems to have fallen on the Thurton family. They lived very close to the infected area, only two or three houses away, and Mrs Thurton had returned from London just two or three days earlier. The suspicion could have been correct: Armstrong notes that the aldermen had received information that plague had broken out in London.

On 16 April, Goodwyn reported three deaths from plague in the previous week, perhaps those from St Augustine's already mentioned. Alderman Anguish was asked to appoint a searcher to view the body of the ostler of the *Bull* in St Stephen's parish to determine whether or not he had died of plague. Over the next few days Peter Witherick agreed to let out his close in Conesford, called the Fryers, for pest-houses: he was paid £14 a year rent. Jaqueline Mansay was appointed a searcher and keeper of the infected among the French-speaking congregation. This is an unusual detail, showing that one person could do both jobs, and also that one person could be keeper for more than one household: in the few other specific mentions of keepers in the Court records, she is appointed to just one. John Denew and Peter Hawtoy were to make sure that she did not go out except when she was being employed as a searcher. The same two men were told to provide a fitting pest-house in case it was thought desirable to remove the infected from their own houses. Clearly this outbreak was mainly among the Walloon community: only one plague death was reported to the court of 23 April, and that was a Frenchman (an unusual detail, normally the nationalities of the dead were not given in the weekly reports).

On 25 April, it was decided that 'the tower called the Great Tower' near Butter Hills should be roofed and fitted up as a pest-house. Two pest-houses were to be built in the same places as they had been the previous year: 'Arnold the carpenter' was appointed to build them and construct the tower roof. Two more died of the plague the following week.

Meanwhile, things were happening in the market town of Wymondham, ten miles south west of Norwich. Plague broke out in April: one family almost certainly plague victims (causes of death are not given in the register) was that of John Thayn: John himself was buried on 2 April, his widow Frances on 10 April, and a son and daughter followed on 18 and 23 April. There were 20 burials in Wymondham in the month of April compared with just four in April of the previous year.

The Norwich authorities took immediate action: at the court of Saturday 30 April, it was ordered that the city gates were to be closed at eight o'clock that night and to stay closed until 1 pm on Monday, and that watches were to be put on the gate.

There were no plague deaths in Norwich in the week ending 7 May, but more preparations were made, ready for immediate action. Two men were appointed as bearers and buriers at four shillings a week (Reynolds and Edwards, forenames not given). Alderman Thomas Atkyn was ordered to disburse, from citizens' money in his hands, cash for the relief of the infected until a rate could be raised. A note added to the entry records shows that he gave out £2. 7s. 8d.

which was later paid back to him by the Treasurer of the Infected. Atkyn and another alderman were asked to find someone to provide food and water for the infected people who were to be brought to the pest-house **that night**.

The aldermen were prepared to take punitive action to enforce the rules as well. The bearers were expected to self-isolate, but just three days later one woman, Anne Bensley, was found to have frequented their company. Her punishment was to be committed to 'a house newly appointed for the pest-house' for the rest of the day. As the court would not do anything to encourage the spread of the plague, the building was presumably still empty, so the day would have been spent in solitary confinement—possibly a punishment especially chosen for a woman who three months earlier had been punished for being 'a scold'!

Meanwhile the plague in Wymondham was taking hold: there were no fewer than 77 burials there in May and 56 in June, ten times the number in the previous summer. Clearly contacts between the town and Norwich threatened the health of the city and the situation was closely watched. One Norwich shoemaker, Nicholas Buntinge, admitted that he had taken on a journeyman shoemaker who had worked near an infected house in Wymondham: the journeyman was told to leave Norwich at once and Buntinge to escort him to Cringleford bridge and make sure that he went! People from Wymondham were only allowed to trade in Norwich if they could produce certificates saying that they had come from uninfected houses. One man, a Wymondham butcher, confessed to the court that his had been forged. Other people who had recently come from Wymondham were interrogated about their certificates—which they no longer had as they had given them to the watchmen at the gates of the city! Three Wymondham butchers disobeyed orders and brought meat into Norwich market to sell at their stalls. A watchman was appointed to stand at each stall and inform everyone that the man was a Wymondham butcher!

However, there was generosity too: over £100 was raised in Norwich for the relief of the infected poor in Wymondham. The Mayors Court book gives the amount raised in each parish, presumably in church on Sunday. Three parishes contributed over £10 each: St Peter Mancroft, St Andrew and St Michael at Plea, all parishes with many wealthy citizens. No other parish came close, the next largest contributors being St John de Sepulchre with £5.10s and St Gregory with £4. At the other end of the scale, nine parishes gave less than a pound each, mainly parishes known from other sources like rate books and hearth tax records to be the poorest areas of the city: St John Timberhill, St Peter Parmentergate, All Saints, St Benedict, St Peter Southgate, St Helen, St Augustine, St Michael at Thorn, St Julian—the last was the smallest contributor at 12s.7½d. The Dutch congregation contributed £5. 12s. 2d, a sum exceeded by only three of the city parishes, but the Walloons were less generous, or less wealthy, contributing only

£1. 16s. 2d.

Certificates like those mentioned were also issued by the Norwich authorities to Norwich people who needed to travel to other towns. The format was:

These are to certify all to whom these presents shall come that the bearer hereof, [person's name], citizen of this city of Norwich, having now occasion to travel into [place name] about his necessary affairs, is resident and dwelling in the parish of [parish name] in the said city, and that as well the house of the said [person's name] wherein he now dwelleth, as the whole parish aforesaid are free and hath not yet been touched with the contagious sickness of the plague.

This bore the seal of the Mayor.

Meanwhile the aldermen kept alert. Members of the Mason family, who had been shut up in their Norwich house for five weeks, were set at liberty. The following week the house of 'a Frenchman', which had been shut up for more than nine weeks was opened as all the people in it were well: this could be the Decore or Latrye house, if they were indeed Walloons.

Three weeks at the end of June and beginning of July saw no deaths from plague. The weekly report of 9 July recorded the first deaths from plague since 30 April. Three people had died in St Margaret's parish in the yard where Luke Hill formerly lived, and a further five had died outside the walls, presumably in Heigham. The dead are not named, but the St Margaret's burial register shows they were all the children of Luke Hill himself, Francis and Luke being buried on 6 July and Anne the following day.

The Court took swift and decisive action: on 6 July , they ordered that a rate be raised, and a searcher was appointed, Margaret Banister. She was placed at Luke Hill's yard and was to be paid 4s. 6d. a week, and two pence for every body she searched; bearers and buriers and watchmen were also put in place. As a further precaution, the schools in Heigham and West Wymer were ordered to be dissolved, a very localized form of lockdown. Three days later, the bearers were told to nail up the doors of infected houses: Arnold the carpenter was ordered to provide nails, board and hammer for the purpose.

Those who had died in St Margaret's had been living in the house of Robert Howse the younger and a watchman was set at his gate. The court sent one of the city marshals to see Howse and to tell him that, if he did not consent to the nailing up of his doors, the Mayor himself would come down and see it done. Howse was truculent, repeating that he would not allow his door to be nailed up, saying he would be glad if the Mayor did come, and adding, 'What, will Mr Mayor make my house a pesthouse or will he starve me?'

The City Assembly met on 15 July, when plague deaths were small but rising

*Houses by St Gregory's churchyard in the early twentieth century (NRO, MS 177).*

(eight had been reported to the Mayor's Court on 9 July). The Assembly ordered that 'pesthouses' be built on the property of Alderman Richard Harman: as always, they were happy to leave it to the aldermen to sort out the actual details. Seven people died of the plague in the week ending 16 July. One was a Mr Leskany of St Martin at Oak: his widow was removed to the pest-house on 21 July. On the same day, Elias Philippo was asked to provide necessaries for its inhabitants. The following week saw nine plague deaths. When the court was told that the son of William Callow in St Benedict's was sick, a watchman was set at his door until it was known whether he had the plague or not. Four more died in the following week. Seven parishes (including three suburbs) were behind with their payments to the fund for the infected. Mr Smith of St Martin at Palace asked the Mayor if he had ordered that there be no ringing or chiming at burials. The Mayor replied that he would not meddle with sextons or clerks, but he hoped that the chimes would be short to prevent people gathering.

Four more people died of plague in the week ending 6 August. Widow Hill who was in the pest-house was permitted to go back to the yard where she had formerly lived. Her removal was to be between nine and ten [not said if this is morning or evening] and a watchman was appointed to ensure she stayed in her house. A second rate was raised for the infected poor. On 13 August, five plague deaths were reported to the Mayor's court, and two people, the wife of Richard Brockdell and widow Cuckson, were sent to the pest-house.

There were other hints of trouble at this time: John Bromely was ordered to be whipped and sent to the Bridewell for resisting a watchman appointed by the Mayor to watch his house, and for abuse to an alderman. On 12 July, it was decided to empty the two towers of the Brazen Gates and turn one into a prison 'for turbulent persons in this time of infection'. Eight days later, the Court ordered that the tower between the pest-house and Ber Street gates be turned into a prison 'to punish such Refractory infected persons as shalbe thither Comitted'. Two men were reported to the Court for violently resisting the shutting up of the Gates. Tempers were clearly becoming frayed under the pressures of enforced lockdown.

The usual measures were agreed upon and John Campe was ordered to kill all the dogs and cats he found between St Gregory's church and the 'further end' of Heigham: he was to get two pence for each one. Meanwhile, in Yarmouth the authorities took steps to enforce a partial lockdown within their town. Noting that most fruit sold there came from Norwich, they ordered that it could not be sold in 'small shops' but only on the Market.

In July, apparently for the first time, articles 'for the ordering of persons and places infected with the plague' were drawn up by the Norwich Court. The actual Orders are not given in the court record: no doubt they were very similar to those issued in 1637 and described below.

It was also ordered that a watchman attend at the Great Hospital during the plague to keep out people who usually came there to buy victuals: their supplies were now to be given to them outside the gate and in the watchman's presence. None of the elderly poor inside, people the twenty-first century would describe as *vulnerable*, could leave except with due cause, and then only with the permission of the Keeper of the hospital. Anyone going out without permission was to be put in the stocks for two hours and to miss their next meal, the food being sent instead to the poor in the House of Correction. The watchman was to be one of the poor in the hospital—and if the watchman was negligent he too would be set in the stocks and miss his next meal! In these ways, *shielding* was provided for the infirm inhabitants.

*The Great Hospital: its vulnerable inhabitants practised self-isolation, like a modern-day care home.*

Deaths from plague continued to be reported: 20 Aug (5), 27 Aug (4), 3 Sept (14), 10 Sept (4), 17 Sept (6). Francis Grene was appointed to watch and provide for the infected, and paid five shillings a week, widow Spreagle was appointed searcher. Some of the others were discharged from their offices. A third rate was made for the relief of the infected. On 24 September, the court heard that five had died of plague in the previous week. They gave liberty to several people hitherto confined to their houses. One group was from St Martin's parish: widow Remers and her child, widow Crome and her child, Aldrich and his child and the maid that kept widow Crome. The widow Dowart of St Gregory's was also allowed to go free. The others were from unidentified parishes: they were Richard Powell with his wife, children and keeper, widow Myhill, her children and keeper.

The weekly figures showed the plague was in decline. Mortality rates in October were: 1 Oct (6), 8 Oct (6), 15 Oct (1), 22 Oct (2). A fourth rate was raised. Henry Church and his family were allowed out after a month self-isolating. The last week of October and the four weeks of November saw the number of plague burials dwindle: there were none in the first two weeks of December, and one in each of the last two weeks of the year. A total of 114 plague burials were recorded during the calendar year, a mild outbreak by the standards of 1603 or 1665-6, but tragic for the families involved. Blomefield (and Armstrong following him) attributes the small number of fatalities to the actions taken by the aldermen: 'such wise precautions were immediately taken as to put an effectual stop to the spreading of the contagion'.

There were no deaths from plague in January, February or early March 1632. It came back then, two deaths in week ending 21 March , one the following week, none on 7 April but three on 14 April.

On 14 April, the Mayor's Court appointed a watchman to watch and provide 'necessaries' (lavatories) for the infected houses in St Saviour's. This entry is the only clue I have seen to help answer the question school pupils always ask (adults presumably being too 'polite' to do so): what did those isolated in infected houses do about going to the toilet? Very many Norwich houses were in yards with a shared convenience, so the question is an extremely pertinent one.

The carpenter was again employed to work on the pest-houses, but the deaths did not rise beyond about one a fortnight in June, and there were none after that or indeed in the following years: the city had entered a plague-free period.

The difficulties of raising money to pay for the expenses caused by the plague are illustrated by several entries in the Mayor's Court in the spring of 1632, and show that the responsibility for actually collecting the cash lay with overseers of the poor in each parish, whom the Court now decided to pursue. On 18 April, four overseers of St Martin at Palace agreed to pay their fines 'for not gathering up money for the Infected'. Three days later, Christopher Curson handed in the ten shillings he was fined for the same offence: 7s. 6d. of it was returned to him. On 25 April, two overseers from St Gregory's parish were fined ten shillings each for failure to collect money for the infected. On 2 May, Matthew Morley promised to pay three shillings that he, Roger Gooch and others had failed to collect for the infected poor from an unspecified parish.

In April 1632, a man named Johannes Puncteus showed the Mayor's Court a royal warrant to sell medicines 'in this or any other city'. Puncteus was a French 'professionary physic' who sold powders and balsams, and who was also involved in the theatre; Charles Bastide sums him up as 'a French quack'[3]. That is just an opinion, of course, but some of his activities may indeed have been dubious: when he was in Edinburgh ten years later, one of his assistants was arrested for robbery.

Preparations for the plague season continued in May, concentrating on the pest-house. On 14 May, two bearers and a searcher were chosen for it. Two more houses were ordered to be built alongside the two already existing: they were to be fenced in with boards. Three days later, a committee of aldermen were asked to view the pest-houses, think about their windows—and to think about 'how, where and in what manner' they could be fenced in. They were to arrange for Arnold the carpenter to build the fence.

There was relatively little plague in the city in the next few years, with no plague deaths at all recorded in 1633 or 1634. (Armstrong records that in 1634 'the plague broke out again in St Augustine's parish, but never arrived to any considerable extent', but he is in error). Blomefield tells us that it was actually in September 1636 that plague erupted in St Augustine's parish: this does not show up in the parish burial register, which records no burials at all in that month, and no burials in 1636 are recorded as being from plague. Of 29 burials in the parish in 1637, just four are noted as being from plague, so that, assuming the recording is reliable, the outbreak was very minor. Blomefield records that the now-usual precautions were taken including the appointment of searchers, one of whom reported the kind of uncertainties about an individual case that must have occurred quite often: she had looked at a body that was covered with 'spots black and blue', but she still had doubts about the cause of death: 'she saith she dare not say upon her oath that it is not of the plague nor that it is of the plague'.

This outbreak of plague was contained, although occasional deaths occurred into 1638: the highest number of deaths were in May 1637, peaking at fifteen or sixteen in a week. In June 1637, the city authorities told Framlingham Gawdy, Thetford Justice of the Peace and former sheriff of the county, that, although the sickness had increased, he could safely attend the Assizes in the city. A report in the autumn said that just three plague deaths had occurred in the previous week.

The authorities were always on the alert for possible danger. In June and July 1633, for example, three groups of players were paid for *not* playing in the city. In 1636, when plague was raging in London and Newcastle, the authorities in Yarmouth and Norwich worked together to try and keep the infection out. Some Yarmouth gates were closed and all the others watched. No one was allowed to go on board any ship from Holland or London in Yarmouth Haven. The Norwich authorities wrote to those in Yarmouth on 1 September:

The times do give us occasion to desire your best aid and assistance, that by the help and goodness of Almighty God, these two corporations of Norwich and Yarmouth, being yet free from the contagion of the plague, may, by God's blessing, be so continued. And therefore we desire, if it may stand with your liking, that all wherrymen that take in any goods or passengers in your town for Norwich, may be compelled to take in at one and the self same place, and not elsewhere. And that none of them be permitted to take in any passengers that come from beyond the seas, from London, Newcastle, or other places infected, or feared to be infected, without a certificate from the worships. And that you would please to cause some officer to make known to all wherrymen that shall come from your town to this city, that they land no goods or passengers at any other place in this city, than at the common staithe in this city, to the end that they may be there examined, and such inquiries be made concerning them as shall be thought fit; because we are now giving order to our wherrymen here, that they observe the same order in this place. And in this doing, we shall account ourselves very much obliged to you, and will be ready to accommodate you in like performance, when you have cause to require the same.

On 3 September, the Yarmouth bailiffs responded:

Your letter of the first of this instant, we have received. And accordingly have ourselves, in person, strictly charged our wherrymen in general that they neither take into, nor deliver out of, the wherries any manner of goods or passengers, but at one certain known place in this town, namely the usual wherry quay; and not any unknown or suspected passengers without our privity. And that they observe the like (according to the contents of your letter) for your city, namely at the common staithe. We heartily thank you for your good care taken herein, and recommended unto us; wherein we have hitherto been careful, and intend for the future (God willing) not to be wanting in conjoining our best help and endeavour for preventing thereof. Neither do we know at present, thanks be given to the Lord, any in this town infected, saving that this week one only person died, who was suspected thereof, and as yet none else of the family sick. With our prayers to the Almighty God, that he will be pleased to stay his hand where it is, and grant a general preservation to the whole kingdom, if it be his blessed will.

It was important to maintain links between Yarmouth and Norwich as the city depended on the supply of cheap herrings from Yarmouth to feed poor families, as we shall see during the 1665-6 outbreak. Yarmouth documents supply an example of an alderman behaving there badly at this time, taking advantage of the situation to line his own pocket. In the days before refrigeration, Yarmouth needed to bring into the town vast quantities of salt in order to preserve the fishing catch. At this date, this was normally brought in from the north-east. However, there was a serious outbreak of plague in Newcastle and it was too risky to bring ships and sailors in to Yarmouth from such a badly infected town. The Yarmouth aldermen decided to import from Europe and sent one of their number, Alderman Horth, to negotiate with the Privy Council for the appropriate licence. However, he secured this not on behalf of the town of Yarmouth but in his own name, thus standing to make huge profits on the business. The matter led to years of legal wrangling: eventually the town won their case and Alderman Horth was deprived of his office as punishment. I have seen no record of any such self-interest in a Norwich alderman, but, as in any crisis, there may have been a minority willing to profit from the misfortunes of others.

During the 1637 outbreak, the Norwich Mayor's Court issued a general set of regulations designed to control the plague. These 'Orders for the Infected', were issued on 13 May 1637 and repeated word for word on 22 August 1638:

1. Imprimis, that there shall be a meeting of the Justices of Peace and Aldermen of this City in the council chamber of this city every Wednesday in the afternoon at two o'clock.

2. Item that every Justice of the Peace and Alderman shall at every such meeting inform themselves by all means what parishes and houses are at the time of such Assembly infected.

3. Item they shall cause to be appointed in every parish as well infected as not infected certain persons to view the bodies of all such as shall die before they be suffered to be buried and to certify the Minister of the church and churchwardens. Or other principal officers or their substitute of what probable disease the said persons died.

4. Item the houses of which there shall die any of the plague being so certified by the viewers or otherwise known or where it shall be understood that any person remained sick of the plague be closed upon all parts during the time of restraint namely six weeks after the sickness in the same house ceased.

5. Item that watchmen be appointed who must be sworn to attend and watch the several infected houses and apprehend any person that shall come out of their house contrary to the order of any Justice of the Peace or Alderman and the same persons be imprisoned in the stock.

6. Item some special mark shall be made and fixed to the doors of every of

the infected houses and where such houses shall be inns or alehouses the signs shall be taken down and some cross or mark as aforesaid set upon the door.

7. Item such as are or shall be appointed keepers buriers and searchers or to have anything to do with persons or hoses infected shall not go abroad the streets or put themselves into any company without some mark on their upper garment or bearing a red wand in their hands. And always in their going from place to place to go next to the channel.

8. Item that the Officer for Certificates shall weekly enquire diligently of the searchers the clerks of the parishes and others especially such as are sworn to the end he may make a true certificate weekly of the just and certain number of persons dying of the plague.

9. Item that the clothes and bedding of persons dying of the infection be buried burned or very well aired and if the owners of the same be poor then the same to be recompensed out of the taxations.

10. Item if any person shall break or contempt any of the orders aforesaid or any other orders by the Mayor, justices and aldermen lawfully devised then every such offender shall be punished by imprisonment or if there shall be cause by binding them over before the Lords of the Privy Council.

11. Item that such schools as are near to any place infected shall be suppressed as time shall give occasion.

12. Item that the aldermen of every ward in this city shall take care that there be no unnecessary concourse or assembly of people within this city for any purpose or occasion whatsoever.

13. Item that every alderman do duly examine the disbursements of the overseers to the infected and make the warrants to the treasurers for payment of the same so as there be care had.

14. Item all persons dying of the infection to be buried in the morning before sun rising or in the evening after sun setting and that no chiming of bells or concourse of people be permitted at such burials.

15. Item every alderman is desired to give such further orders to all inferior officers as they shall upon every occasion think fit for preventing of every inconvenience that may anyway occasion the increase of the infection.

Surviving reports show a further small outbreak in 1638, with four plague deaths in the week ending 24 April, seven in the week ending 14 May, four in the week ending 25 June, five in the week ending 13 August, two in the week ending 20 October and three in a week ending about 10 November. Reports do not survive for the intervening weeks.

The city authorities had long realised that overcrowding was an important factor in the spread of plague, and the City Quarter Sessions occasionally intervened. In 1631, Mary Newman of Mancroft Ward (parish not named) was accused of crowding her house with poor people: she had taken four families into her house, which was not fit for more than two people, and did not even have a 'house of ofis' [lavatory]. Her accusers indicated one reason for the case: all these poor families were likely to become chargeable to the parish. Mary was not a very satisfactory person in general: she had failed to pave the street in front of her house, and had not been to church for three months. In 1637, Thomas and Mary Stalworthy of St Swithin's were charged with 'overcharging and pestering their houses with poore people'—they had taken in people from the Lazar House. There were 13 families—46 people in all—under the one roof, and 'some of them keep swine in their dwelling houses'. These cases were extreme examples since the landlords were prosecuted, but many people lived in conditions that were not a great deal better.

There was no major outbreak for many years after 1638: Armstrong notes an outbreak in 1646 in Norwich and Dereham 'but its effects were very inconsiderable'. The authorities perhaps hoped it had at last gone away, or at least that they were on top of the problem: the weekly record of deaths/burials given to the Mayor's court was stopped in the 1640s. However, there was still one very serious outbreak to come.

## PEST-HOUSES

We have already mentioned one refinement in the prevention of an outbreak of plague: the introduction of pest-houses. People suffering from the plague might be removed from their own homes and put into the pest-house, where they would be isolated, together with other plague sufferers, and remain there until they had either died or had recovered—and had ceased to be infectious. Orders issued by the Privy Council in 1665 required 'each town … to provide some convenient place remote from the same, where a pest-house, huts or sheds may be erected.' In fact, many towns had such temporary structures thirty years or more before that date. A few more permanent pest-houses even exist today, such as at Odiham, Hampshire, and Shalford, Surrey, but the ones built in Norwich were not intended to last for more than one year of plague. The first reference to a pest-house I have seen is in 1583, when the Privy Council recommended one be built in London. The first one in the capital was actually constructed in 1594, provincial cities eventually following in London's wake.[4]

Pest-houses were a common feature of the seventeenth century fight against plague after the 1620s. In Great Yarmouth, for example, 'cotes' on the Denes were fitted up as pest-houses in 1631, and in 1637 two old lazar or leper houses outside the north gate were adapted as pest-houses, wood from 'a little house in the fort by the seaside' being used for the purpose. Both sites were outside the town walls of the borough.

The first mention of a pest-house in the Norwich documents appears to be in 1626 when the Privy Council suggested that the city might forego the Mayor's feast for that year and spend the money on building a pest-house instead: however, the aldermen convinced the Privy Council that they should hold their feast as usual.

The first record of actually building any pest-houses comes in 1630, when six were ordered to be built on Butter Hills, just inside the city alongside the city walls: this is the area between Carrow Hill and Ber Street, an open area where the city walls are still well preserved, with several towers, the most notable being the Black Tower. The structures were only temporary: in the following year, it was decided to erect two pest-houses where the previous year's buildings had been, and to re-roof the Black Tower for use as a pest-house. The carpenters' bill for work, board and timber at the Pest-house and the Black Tower survives, giving the impression of very temporary structures. The total for wood was £13 13s. 0d., £3 6s. of which was at the Black Tower (boards, planks, posts and rails), the rest at the Pest-house (the same, also deals, three doors, and 160 feet of new board for partitions). The total spent on labour for both projects was £1 11s. 0d, the men being paid at 1s. 6d. a day.[5]

Although there is nothing about it in the records of the Mayor's Court, the towers may have been used for the purpose of isolation as early as 1603, when a woman is recorded in the St Peter Mancroft burial register as having been 'sent' to 'a tower', where she died.Pest-houses came into their own in 1666, with a guard house built near them in March to ensure compliance.

Figures in the *London Gazette* record 89 deaths there, about half a dozen a week on average, peaking in July with twenty deaths there in one week. The overall figures of plague between October 1665 and October 1666 record 217 people as having died in the pest-house. There must have a reasonable number of people there at any one time, but 90% of deaths still occurred in people's houses, so the inhabitants of the pest-houses made up a very small percentage of the infected in the city.

A further refinement came in June 1666, when huts and booths were ordered to be erected to act as 'cleansing houses' after people were removed from the pest-house: presumably they lived there for the remainder of the period of quarantine.

It is possible that some informal pest-houses did exist elsewhere. Writing in

the eighteenth century, Matthew Brettingham noted that in 1579 'the Inhabitants
… built Pest Houses at every Gate of the City to remove the Infected Poor to.' He
is presumably referring to the lazar houses, used as institutions for the sick poor,
which may have had some temporary accommodation for this purpose. Unlike
the pest-houses proper, these institutions were just *outside* the city walls. In the
1660s, a petition by the churchwardens of the parish for a house for an 85-year-
old man describes the St Augustine's lazar house site as 'Pest House Yard', while
Brettingham's document describes the Pest-house there as 'now in ruins', so it
seems there was some building on the site that was regarded as having been a
pest-house.[6]

Descendants of pest-houses, known as isolation hospitals, were common in
nineteenth century and later Britain. The twenty-first century version would be
the Nightingale Hospitals, constructed specifically to house Covid patients. In
a sense, every hospital has had to create the equivalent of a pest-house, wards
where Covid patients are rigorously kept separate from the other patients: a
task of far greater complexity than putting up temporary accommodation in an
isolated spot at the edge of the city.

**Notes**

1     NRO, NCR 26f/6, dated 12 July 1625.

2     NRO, NCR 21b/6.

3     Charles Bastide, *The Anglo-French détente in the seventeenth century* (1875) p.236.

4     Slack, *op. cit.* p.214. As the 1583 Privy Council pointed out, such houses already existed in cities
      on the Continent.

5     NRO, NCR 18a/13.

6     NRO, DN/EST 52/3; NCR 12e/3.

# The Last Great Outbreak
# 1665-1667

THERE was an extremely serious outbreak of plague in England in 1665, the year of London's 'Great Plague'. In the capital nearly 100,000 people out of a population of 400,000 may have died. The Lord Mayor of London issued a new set of rules emphasising the need for self-isolation and social distancing—women who acted as searchers were forbidden to work as shopkeepers or laundrymaids, and each infected house was to have one or two watchmen to make sure nobody came in or out. The dead were to be buried before sunrise or after sunset, and graves were to be at least six feet deep—presumably the origin of the metaphor for death 'six feet under', and of the (incorrect) belief held by many today that burials have to be of this depth. Not all these rules were more severe than those of the twenty-first century—entertainments and shows were banned, but not all places where people gathered: only those ale-houses and coffee-shops that were judged to be 'unruly' were to be closed down.

The plague outbreak of 1665 was not confined to the capital. It erupted in Yarmouth at the end of May, peaking at 96 deaths in the last week of August and 100 in the first week of September. In fact, the system was overwhelmed—no burials are recorded for two weeks in August. As the whole of Yarmouth, in sharp contrast to Norwich, was a single parish it is impossible that there were no deaths at all in this period, so the recording must be at fault—perhaps connected with the fact that the parish clerk, Robert Parr, became sick himself, being buried on 8 September. The outbreak declined in the autumn but continued on a small scale into early 1666, the five plague deaths there in mid-February being the last.

In Norwich, there was some plague in 1665, but it was 1666 when the city was severely hit. The city authorities saw plague raging elsewhere and took steps to try and keep Norwich safe. On 19 July 1665, the Mayor's Court ordered that chains be drawn across the river between the boom towers to prevent boats and keels coming up the river from Yarmouth. A boat with three or four people in was to be kept near Carrow both day and night to note what boats came from Yarmouth and to take the names of any people arriving without bills of health. Two days later, passenger coaches and carts to or from London were prohibited. Wealthy merchant Onias Philippo was allowed to send just one cart to London a week, but he broke the regulation by sending three carts to London in just one day. No passengers or goods from London or Yarmouth were to be admitted 'without certificates under seal'. Despite the precautions, the plague devastated the city, with 203 deaths in one week in August: fortunately this turned out to be the peak.

The authorities continued to lay down further rules in 1666 even as plague raged in the city. Those of April 1666 show that the city was so small that people could even consider individual cases. The Court noted that the sickness was 'near' the house of John Osborne in St Julian's parish. His servant, John Bucknam, was staying with his parents at the time and he was told to stay there 'till the danger be over', unless his master showed good cause to the contrary.

Even before, on 28 March, the Court ordered that watch houses be erected as near to the pest-houses as possible, and a guard with firelocks placed there to prevent people visiting the pest-house—and to keep in those who were inside. Anybody coming close was to be told to walk on or ride by, and the guards were told 'if any shall offend therein to fire upon them'. On 7 April it was arranged that these guards should be paid out of the Hamper [petty cash], or, if there were not sufficient funds there, their wages were to be charged on the chamberlain or foreign receiver.

In May 1666, the Court ordered that carriers from Colchester, where the plague was 'very great' must not bring any wool or other commodities into Norwich. On 3 June a committee of three aldermen was formed to provide workmen and materials to erect huts and booths in Butter Hills to act as 'cleansing houses' for people when they were removed from the pesthouse.

Meetings of the Mayor's Court throughout the summer of 1666 were concerned with the usual two problems: how to control the spread of the infection and how to pay for these measures. On 9 July, it was ordered that the Grammar school and all other schools of reading or writing be forthwith dissolved until further notice. On 16 July, Francis Deane of St Julian's was employed to nail up the doors of 'such houses as are or shall be infected', and paint red crosses on their doors: while doing this, he was to carry a red wand. He was paid 4d for each door. At the same time, Samuel Viall of St Michael Coslany was appointed to kill dogs, cats and swine found in the city streets, and to bury them in the bottom of the Castle Ditches or the City Ditches. He was to have 3d for 'every dog and swyne' he killed (nothing is said of any payment for the cats). The vulnerable were once more considered—the rules for shielding at the Great Hospital first set out in 1631 were reissued. Disorder was feared: on 19 September, it was ordered that 'five or six persons be engaged to punish such persons as being shut in shall break up their boards or doors or be refractory to the orders of the court concerning infected houses or the pesthouse'.

Meanwhile a 'double rate for the infected poor' was raised, with another rate following soon after. The Mayor transferred £100 of money belonging to the city's corn stock fund. The Bishop of Norwich gave £200 towards relief of the infected poor. City churchmen Robert Harmer and Richard Ireland lent or gave money; Mrs Suckling of Bracondale, just outside the city, gave £5; one Londoner sent 40 shillings; the inhabitants of Mundham, Seething and Thwaite gave £18 3s. 6d., while the two Mattishall parishes contributed £19.10s: these were probably the result of a brief (appeal) read out in the village churches. Norwich put an appeal for funds into the *London Gazette* on 27 September: 'the city is in a very deplorable condition, by reason of the continued raging of the sickness, and is become a very fit object of charity'.

The city spent over £8,000 on measures to alleviate the plague, up to £200 a week. In July, the Town Clerk, Thomas Corie, went to London in person to try to raise money, and also to obtain the services of two medical men named Hargrave and Boghurst. I have not been able to find a reference to Hargrave. William Boghurst was an apothecary in St Giles-in-the-Fields, London, who had made his reputation during the Great Plague there in 1665. He blamed the plague on the stinking open drains, and criticised the practices of doctors who bled patients and lanced swollen buboes.

Sadly, the mission was a failure: the men did not leave London. Some London surgeons did come to help, however: the Court Book of 14 November records that over £30 was spent on medicines that a Mr Fiffe and other London surgeons had provided to help the infected poor of the city. The aldermen paid the bill and gave the surgeons a gratuity as a token of their gratitude.

Another precaution was to move the Market out of the city, presumably to encourage social distancing. It was held on the Town Close, then an open area outside St Stephen's gates. This meant that country traders need not bring their goods into the city, and it was hoped that this would 'prevent the scattering of that Noysome pestilence'. It was the county magistrates who first suggested this, writing to the Mayor of Norwich on 12 July to say that this would enable county folk to sell their wares without having to come into the city.[1]

On 7 April 1666, it was ordered that Heigham, St Benedict's, St Giles' and St Stephen's Gates be closed on the following Tuesday and watchmen set there to prevent poor people going out for the funeral of 'Serjaunt Waller's son'. These gates are on the western side of the city: presumably the funeral took place in Heigham parish church (the parish records for the period do not survive). Marshals were also to go to the Waller family's house to prevent a crowd gathering there. Sergeants were city officials working for the Mayor and sheriffs. There is nothing to suggest why this particular funeral should merit such a specific mention in the Mayor's Court book, but it is a good illustration of the steps the authorities could take to preserve social distancing by preventing a crowd gathering. There were many similar instances. For example, in September 1666, the Bishop of Ely announced that the annual fairs of St Luke and St Audrey, normally held at Ely in October, would not be held, 'plague continuing very dangerous at Cambridge, Peterborough and other places near Ely'. In the previous year, Thomas Throckmorton of Bungay had complained that men from Yarmouth were trading at Bungay Fair in 1665, at a time when plague was rife in Yarmouth.[2]

The outbreak raged for more than twelve months. As always, the great majority of deaths were in the summer months, but there were some deaths in the autumn and even the winter. In 1666, the peak week was the third week of August, with 203 plague deaths. It then declined, with a rise in mid-September when thirty houses were newly affected. There were 58 plague deaths in the last week of October, and 31 in the week of 24 November. There was even a small revival in 1667, with two deaths in the week ending 20 March and four in the first week of June. After 8 June 1667 there were no more plague deaths in Norwich—ever! On Thursday 19 September 1667 a public day of thanksgiving was held in the city with sermons read in every church.

The Town Clerk, Thomas Corie, sent the plague figures to London every week, his accompanying letters capturing the tensions of the time:

| | |
|---|---|
| 4 July 1666 | 'the plague grows fast among us' |
| 18 July | 'the plague encreaseth daily' |
| 5 September | 'I fynde some abatement of the number (but a dispersing into fresh houses) of the plague' |
| 19 September | 'though there hath been some little decrease of the sickness for 2 or 3 weekes yet this weeke is an increase, and above 30 new houses' |
| 3 October | 'I can now more cheerfully send you a Byll of Mortality by reason of a considerable decrease, but wee have almost every day erruptions of new howses, which abates our joye' |
| 10 October | 'our number is twoe more in the city, though 4 lesse at the pesthouse, and to deale freely with you, it spreads much into new houses.' |
| 24 October | 'blessed be god wee have had a decrease of 59 of the plague this weeke and doe hope the coole season will beget a daily abatement.' |
| 7 November | 'Wee have (blessed be god) some little abatement this weeke in our byll of Mortality, but are full of feares still in respect of the daily irruptions of new howses'. |

28 November      'the plague blessed be god decreaseth'
20 March 1667   'we have but 2 dead of the plague this weeke'.

The London Gazette recorded weekly deaths from plague in Norwich from the week ending 13 June, when there were 18 plague deaths. The number rose inexorably to 65 in the week ending 18 July, then more than doubled to 130 in the following week. Numbers continued to rise until the week ending 22 August when 201 plague deaths were recorded. The number then fell to 180 in the following week, and for the next four weeks there were 135 to 147 deaths each week. There were 139 plague deaths in Norwich in the week ending 26 September, the London Gazette reporting that 'this city is in a very deplorable condition, by reason of the continued raging of the sickness'.

Plague deaths fell to 100 at the beginning of October, rising again with a second smaller 'spike' of 127 in the week ending 17 October. There was a dramatic fall to 68 in the following week, and the numbers fell to the low thirties in November. In the week ending 28 November, the London Gazette recorded 'we have this week (God be praised) a great decrease of the sickness': there were just fifteen plague deaths in the week. Deaths continued at these low figures throughout December, after which the Norwich figures were no longer entered into the paper.

There is a difference between these figures and those presented to the Mayor's Court relating to epidemics in the earlier outbreaks: those were given only to the aldermen, whereas those in the Gazette were, of course, in the public domain. Perhaps not that many people read the newspaper, but it could well have been available in coffee houses, even read aloud to those present, a seventeenth century equivalent to those people in the twenty-first century who gather in public houses to watch football matches shown on expensive subscription channels that they could not afford to watch at home.

I have looked at the numbers of burials for each year in the 1660s for a sample of twelve parishes: St Michael at Plea, St Gregory, St Martin at Palace, St George Tombland, St James Pockthorpe, Saints Simon and Jude, St Peter Mancroft, St Stephen, St Paul, St Saviour, St Julian and St Benedict. The figures show that there were some plague burials in 1665 (for example, three in St Gregory) and some in 1667 (five in St James Pockthorpe), but the greatest number of deaths was in the year of 1666, the highest burial numbers being 283 in St Stephen, 188 in St Julian and 176 in St Peter Mancroft.

The number of plague burials, with the total number of burials and the number of baptisms for each parish between 3 October 1665 and 3 October 1666 were published in Norwich Records (1736): see Appendix Four. These figures are not completely reliable, if only because the plague continued beyond

3 October 1666 in some parishes, but make a good starting point. I have added the figures of population totals for each parish from the first census of the city, that of 1693. These figures enable us to see the parts of the city worst affected by the 1666 plague in terms of deaths as a percentage of the 1693 population rather than total deaths.

The eight parishes worst hit (those where the number of burials exceeded 10% of the 1693 population) are: St Peter Southgate, St Etheldreda, St Julian, St Peter Parmentergate, St Michael at Thorn, All Saints, St Margaret and St James. This suggests the plague had most effect on a particular area of Norwich, that along King Street where most of these parishes lie. These may also be among the parishes that house the poorest in the city: six of them are recorded by Walter Rye as being among those fourteen parishes with one or no houses at all rated at four pence in the first surviving Norwich rate book

*The porch of St Peter Parmentergate, the worst-hit parish in the 1665-6 outbreak.*

(1633-4), and this would probably be seven if St Etheldreda was not omitted from his analysis of the rate book. At the other end of the scale, the eight parishes least badly hit (where burials were 2% or less of the 1693 population) were St Benedict, St Andrew, St Gregory, St Michael at Plea, St George Tombland, St Helen, St Edmund and St Saviour.

Taking three parishes of much the same size (each with a population of around 900 in 1693) shows how greatly the death rates between parishes varied: St Andrew recorded just twelve plague burials, St Giles recorded 66, while St Michael at Thorn recorded no less than 202! Of course, there were family tragedies even in the lightly-hit parishes: in St Giles, to take just one example, Thomas Wilsher lost four young sons in twelve days in June 1666.

It would seem self-evident that the poor suffered during a plague to a much greater extent than the better off. The rich could always leave for their second homes. Those who stayed could self-isolate far more easily in their larger houses than could poor families crowded together in one or two rooms. The city recognised the link between overcrowding and plague and took steps against the worse cases. Over a century ago, Hudson and Tingey in their 'Selected Records of the City of Norwich' put the matter succinctly, albeit in terms we would not use today: 'during the later visitations of the disease it attacked the poorest class almost exclusively, sweeping away the dregs of the population'.[3]

*St Clement's parish church: there were only sixteen plague burials here in 1665-6.*

To put flesh on the figures, I have looked at a large number of original parish registers for the period. Several parish registers record the start of the plague. A note in St Benedict's register for 1666 says 'The plague began the 11th of May'. At St James Pockthorpe, the register also notes in May 1666 'the plague began', and in March 1667, 'the plague ended'. In All Saints, the first plague burial was John Gilman on 5 July 1666, the last, George, the son of George Leeds on 11 March 1667. However, the plague at St Lawrence began and ended rather earlier: a note in the burial register records: 'buried of the plague from November 3 1665 to December 10 1666: 72'.

In All Saints, the burial of Gilman was soon followed by a whole family. Robert Rawlings and his son were buried on 16 July, followed by four further Rawlings children, including an unbaptised and unnamed daughter, all on 24 July. There were nine burials in the churchyard on just one day, 29 August. There were 31 burials in September, just two said to be 'clere', falling to 12 in October. The worst was over although there were occasional plague deaths in the parish for a further five months.

The registers record many family tragedies. At St Stephen's, the first three plague deaths were of the same family: Sarah, the daughter of John Style, haberdasher, was buried on 15 May, her brother Samuel on 29 May and John Style himself on 9 June. A child of 'widow' Jackson was buried on 19 July, two more, also unnamed, on 28 and 29 July, and widow Jackson herself, her name finally being revealed to be Margaret, on 3 August.

*The burial register for Norwich St Stephen's, 1666 (NRO, PD 484/2).*

The registers for St Stephen's are exceptionally detailed, giving occupations, marital status and occasionally age. These give a vivid impression of life in Norwich during a time of plague. When someone's house was locked down, inhabitants would include live-in servants and apprentices who would have to take their chances with actual family members, as the households of two blacksmiths in the parish demonstrate. John Jackson buried two of his children and a servant (Elizabeth Mason) between 20 August and 4 September. John Blancher buried his apprentice, Thomas Ellis, on 13 September, and his own son, Ichabod, four days later. Of course, every time there was a further death, the period of isolation would be extended. An extreme example of this was the

Herrington family of St John Sepulchre. Mary Herrington was buried on 9 August 1666, and the remaining members of the family would have been locked into the house on that day. Other family members died between then and 13 October. Any survivors would remain for a further five or six weeks before being given the all-clear: they would have been in isolation (no leaving the house, not even for exercise) for just short of four months, dependent upon a keeper for supplies of food and drink.

Ages are occasionally given, normally when people would be regarded as unusually aged, in this case from their mid-sixties upwards. The oldest victim of the plague I have seen was Robert Browne, aged about 80, buried in St Stephen's on 21 August 1666. The same register records four burials of people in their seventies upwards in the three months of December 1666 to February 1667, but none of these were from plague: presumably, the harsh realities of winter took their normal toll of the aged. At All Saints, the one burial in October 1666 not from plague was that of Francis Swan described as an 'old mayd above 60': that a woman of 60 could be regarded as so exceptionally aged as to be noted in the burial register is a clear indication of how social demography in the seventeenth century differed from that of the twenty-first century.

Plague victims in St Stephen's parish can be looked at in several ways. The first burial indicated as plague was on 15 May 1666, the last on 26 June 1667. During this period, there were 271 plague burials in the parish. In terms of gender, 54% were of females, 39% of males (the remaining 7% are described simply as 'children', no gender given).

**Children**: 141 (52%) of the burials were of children. This clearly marks the plague as being very different than the Covid-19 epidemic in 2020: in the latter case, very few children indeed died of the disease. However, it does not necessarily mean that plague was *more* fatal to children than to adults. In seventeenth century Norwich, as in developng nations in more recent times, the percentage of the population who were children was very much higher than in Britain today—many more children were born and far fewer people lived into old age. Seventy-one of the children are given as female, fifty-two as male. A further eighteen are described as 'a child of ….' with no indication of gender. Two of these eighteen are described as 'unbaptised' suggesting that the other sixteen had been baptised, but the clerk did not have their names to hand, and therefore their gender cannot now be discovered.

If young people were much more likely to die from plague in the sixteenth and seventeenth centuries than from Covid in the present, it is probably true that they *felt* less vulnerable than the old. As Ralph Houlbrooke puts it: 'Not surprisingly, many young people found it more difficult to keep their minds on death and what lay beyond it'. He cites the example of a London teenager, Elizabeth Livingstone, who lived in London in the plague year of 1665: even when there was plague in her father's house, this had little effect on her life of 'gayety and pleasures'. No doubt, many teenagers in Norwich felt the same.[4]

**Women**: 76 of the burials are of women. Only five are described in terms of occupation—two female servants, two female apprentices, and one woman described as 'keeper', discussed elsewhere. All the other women are described in terms of marital status: ten single women, 39 wives and 22 widows. Widowhood might, of course, be a direct result of plague: there are several cases where a man has died of plague, to be followed to the grave, sometimes just two or three days, later by his former wife, now correctly described as 'widow'.

**Men**: 54 of the burials are of men, in most cases their occupation being given. A very small number are described only in terms of marital status: four are called single men, three widowers (perhaps too old to have an occupation, one being described as 'about eighty'). One man is described simply as 'Thomas Messenger junior, married' with no occupation given. This does not imply that he was of a high social status; he was presumably the son of Thomas Messenger senior, a ribbon weaver, who also died of plague.

The most common occupation is weaving, often with further sub-grouping (worsted weaver, lace weaver, ribbon weaver etc): fourteen men fall into this category. The next largest groups were tailors (4) and husbandmen (3). Occupations with just a single plague burial include glazier, ostler, gingerbread maker, innholder, sexton, physician, carpenter and cobbler. Just one burial is of a 'gentleman' and even he is described as a cobbler in the burial entry for one of his children! Plague victims with more unusual trades buried in St Stephen's included John Tonge 'ballad singer' buried on 30 September, and Anne, the wife of John Edwards 'musician', buried on 25 October.

At least one woman paid to be a keeper or watcher herself died of the plague, and we can trace the family history through the burial entries. Robert Seaman died of the plague in late July 1666, probably on the 25th as he was buried at St Stephen's on the 26th. The house was then shut up with the rest of the household inside, and Anne Fenn appointed keeper. Plague continued to kill family members: Mary Cooper, apprentice was buried on 9 August, and Elizabeth, daughter of Robert Seaman, was buried on 11 Aug. Each time there was a death, the quarantine period would have been extended. Anne Fenn, now described as 'keeper of the widow Seaman' caught the plague herself, died, and was buried on 16 August. However, Robert's widow probably did survive: there is no record of her burial in August, September or October 1666. It is possible, however, that she was removed to the pest-house and died there.

*Norwich, St Paul's church, bombed in the Second World War. There were plague burials here from October 1665 to June 1667 (NRO, MC 630/188).*

In the much smaller parish of St John Timberhill deaths attributed to plague were confined to a three-month period, 7 August to 9 November 1666. Fifty-seven people died: 24 adults (twelve men, twelve women) and 33 children (eighteen males, fifteen females), so that, again a little over half of the burials were of children. The parish registers of St John Sepulchre are among the least informative in the city, with no description of age, occupation or relationship. No burials are marked as being of plague victims, but it is still obvious that something terrible happened in the parish in the late summer of 1666: after just two burials between January and May, the figures increased dramatically: two in June, ten in July, 31 in August, 18 in September, 20 in October. Burials then fell: six in November, three in December and then no burials until March 1667.

In St Julian's parish, where the plague also did not strike until 1666, the first deaths were in one family, the children of Thomas Downing: George on 15 April 1666, Robert 26 April, Ann, Margaret and Charles all on 27 April. Thomas himself was buried on 5 May, the register noting that 'he and his five children died all of the sickness'.

At St Paul the first plague death was Samuel Carr on 30 October 1665, the last Joseph, son of Joseph Newparke, on 12 June 1667. The peak day for burials was on 15 October 1666 with four burials all from plague—William Poynter, William Payne, and Dorothy and William Paw. The Paws suffered other deaths: Edmund, son of Robert, on 16 July, Richard Paw on 12 October, Robert and John Paw on 13 October. The Poynters also had other losses: another William Poynter was buried on 28 September, and Mary and Frances Poynter on 14 October.

In St James Pockthorpe, the Joel family were very badly hit in August 1666: Joel Joel was buried on 14 Aug: his first son, also Joel, had predeceased him, buried on 11 August and three more sons followed—James also on 14 Aug and Jacob and John on the following day. Another Joel, John, also died on 15 August and he was followed by his son, George, two days later and by his wife, Mary, on 25 August. Burials at Saints Simon and Jude in Aug/Sep 1666 include four children of John Claxton—Elizabeth on 17 Aug, Sarah on 4 Sep, George on 7 September, Susan on 16 September.

Some parishes had very few plague burials even at the peak of the outbreak. Of eight burials in St Martin at Palace in June and July 1666, just two were plague victims, and one of these actually died in St Paul. However, sometimes every burial was that of a plague victim, such as at St Peter Mancroft in July 1666, where all of the 49 burials are marked as being from plague. One of the 49 victims was Ann Beckett, buried on 7 July. Her case is especially interesting because we have details of the events that occurred while she lay dying of plague (they are revealed in depositions concerning a dispute about her will). As she lay in her chamber 'being visited of the plague of which she died', she saw a friend, Jane Hawes, passing by. Ann threw down her keys to her saying, 'Jane I give you all that I have and desire you to let me have a coffin to bury me in'. Presumably she was desperate to avoid her body being thrown uncoffined into a plague pit: the burial register does not record whether her request was granted. Incidentally, there seems to have been no question of isolating the dying woman: a witness in the case noted that there were 'present at least a dozen people'.

In September 1666 at St Martin at Palace, the one burial NOT of a plague victim was Thomas Firman, who the register records was 'buried cleare Sep 25'. There were thirteen plague victims in the month, six from one family:

| | |
|---|---|
| 5 September | Mary, daughter of John Beake |
| 9 September | Jane, daughter of John Beake |
| 16 September | John, son of John Beake |
| 17 September | Elizabeth, daughter of John Beake |
| 18 September | Sara, daughter of John Beake |
| 19 September | Elizabeth, wife of John Beake. |

Other burials in the parish in September included three members of the Garwood family and two of the Elmes family, so that there were just two plague burials not from one of these three families.

Another parish that distinguished those who were buried from plague from those who were buried 'cleere' was St John Maddermarket. There were fifteen burials in the busiest month, August 1666, twelve from plague and three described as 'cleere'. The first burial to be described as plague was a little earlier: Martha, daughter of John Norgate, was buried on 28 July 1666. She was soon followed by her parents, Ann being buried on 6 August and John on the following day. One unfortunate family suffered six deaths, five members being buried in just four days:

| | |
|---|---|
| 12 August | Island, son of Island Sparke |
| 23 August | Island Sparke |
| 24 August | Mary, daughter of Island Sparke |
| 25 August | Samuel, son of Island Sparke |
| 25 August | Liddiah, daughter of Island Sparke |
| 26 August | Sarah, late wife of Island Sparke. |

The city prison on Guildhall Hill was in the parish of St John Maddermarket, and the register records the burial of Robert Shinkfield 'prisoner out of the Jayle' on 12 October 1666, another victim of the plague. Plague could well have spread like wildfire within such an institution, but the inhabitants appear to have been fortunate: no other burials of prisoners are recorded in the parish register for the period 1665 to 1667. There is one other reference to the burial of a prisoner at this time, not in St John Maddermarket, as one would expect, but in the burial register for St Peter Mancroft: Climbert Lambert 'a prisoner goale' was buried there on 4 April 1665. This was before the main outbreak of plague, and this register does not, in any case, distinguish plague burials from others, so there is

*St John Maddermarket church: plague burials in 1665 included a prisoner from the city gaol.*

no way of knowing if Lambert was another victim: even if he was, two deaths in eighteen months hardly constitutes an outbreak.

There was certainly a fear that prison was a dangerous place to be in time of plague. John Dade was languishing in gaol in Norwich at the time of the 1579 outbreak because of unpaid debts. Two influential friends wrote to the High Sheriff of Norfolk on 29 June asking that he be set free because of the risk: 'how dangerous it is for him in this perilous time of God's visitation to have continuance in Norwich'. Dade was presumably in Norwich Castle, which was the county gaol, rather than the city gaol where the High Sheriff of Norfolk would have no jurisdiction.[5]

It would be interesting to examine burials for other institutions in the city, Norwich Castle prison (for county prisoners rather than city prisoners), the Great Hospital and the Norman's hospital/almshouses (where a large number of poor people lived, according to the 1570 census of the poor). Unfortunately, the burial registers for St Michael at Thorn (for the Castle), St Helen (for the Great Hospital) and St Paul (for the Norman's) do not survive for the sixteenth or seventeenth centuries. Other institutions taking in those too poor or sick to look after themselves included the former lazar houses just outside the city walls and parish poorhouses. A small number of burials from inhabitants of such institutions do occur in burial registers, such as these two from the register for St Clement:

> 9 March 1626: A stranger from the spittle house whose name was not known
> 26 January 1631: A stranger whose name we could not learn died at the lazar house without St Augustine's Gates and was here buried.

In these cases, stranger presumably means 'unknown', not that they were members of the Norwich 'Stranger' community. These burials represent a transient and poorly-recorded group of, perhaps temporary, incomers. The register does not give any cause of death, so it is not known if they were victims of plague.

St Andrew was another parish very lightly touched by this outbreak of plague. The statistics record only 37 deaths in the period October 1665 to October 1666 and, of these, under a third (twelve) were from plague. The parish registers record 29 burials in the whole of 1666, actually seven less than the number in 1665. Although the peak month for burials in the parish in these two years was indeed August 1666, the 'spike' was incredibly small—eight burials. There were 721 deaths from plague in the city of Norwich in August 1666: in St Andrew's parish in that month, there were just eight burials, and not all of these were necessarily from plague: the register does not give any causes of death.

The 1666 plague peaked at different times in different parishes. In St Peter

Mancroft the highest number of burials was in *July*, with 49 burials, falling to 32 in August, 21 in September and 22 in October. In St Julian and St James Pockthorpe, the peak came in *August*. In St Julian there were 64 burials in July, rising to 89 in August and then falling rapidly to just 13 in September and only one in October. In St James Pockthorpe, the burials were very much concentrated in August: there were four burials in July, 36 in August, five in September and four in October. The peak in St Stephen and St Martin at Palace came in *September*. In St Stephen's there were just six burials in July, jumping to 51 in August and then 74 in September, rapidly falling to just thirteen in September, and just one in October. St Martin at Palace, with a much smaller population, saw five plague burials in August, fourteen burials in September, and just two in October. The peak in St Paul's did not come until *October*: there were just three burials in July and four in August. The figure rose to 14 in September and then jumped to 27 in October, falling back to four in November.

The Society of Friends (Quakers) began maintaining its own registers in 1665. The group was very small at first and several years often passed without a death being recorded. The record of seven deaths in 1666 is therefore very suggestive, (although causes of death are not given), especially as they came from just three families. Joseph Whittlock 'departed' this life on 31 August, Thomas Allen on 13 November and his widow Margaret Allen the following day. The other four deaths came in the Buddery family: Susan Buddery, wife of Thomas Buddery, died on 30 July, two daughters, Mary and Hagar on 12 August, and a son, Joshua, just two days later. The life of this family can be reconstructed for the records. Thomas Buddery married Susan Rosier at St Mary Coslany on 26 November 1649. Of their children, Mary was born in 1657 and Hagar in 1665, so the daughters were nine and one years old when they died.

A count of **daily burials** in St Julian and St Peter Mancroft, between 16 July and 13 August 1666, shows how different parishes were affected at different times. Burials at St Julian peaked on the four days of 20-23 July, with 41 burials in just four days, and on 6 August when there were 17 burials in one day! The only day in the period on which there were more than three burials at St Peter Mancroft was on 8 August, when there were eleven. Daily burials at St Stephen's reached double figures on two occasions—there were eleven burials on 8 August and again on 11 September.

In sharp contrast, some parishes had very few plague deaths. In several parishes, the number of plague burials throughout 1666 did not reach double figures, for example St Benedict, St Saviour and George Tombland. The total number of plague deaths over the *whole* of 1666 in each of these parishes did not reach the number of burials in the worst *single day* in St Julian or St Stephen!

To get a longer perspective, I have looked at burials for St Peter Mancroft and St Mary Coslany over **several decades** to compare the outbreaks of plague between 1579 and1666. The figures show that at St Peter Mancroft, the 1579 outbreak produced the greatest mortality with 241 burials, followed by 1666 with 176 burials and 1603 with 115 burials. The plagues of the 1620s and 1630s did not have the same dreadful rates of mortality: the year with the highest burial figure in this period being 1626, when there were 59 burials. At St Mary Coslany, the greatest mortality was in 1603, with 80 burials, followed by 1579 with 69 burials. In this parish, the plagues of the 1620s and 1630s, however, were almost as fatal: there were 47 burials in 1626 and 56 in 1637.

I have also looked at the **monthly** rates for these three plague years for St Peter Mancroft, and included a few other years for comparison. These show that in non-plague years burial rates were about the same in the summer as in the winter, but that in plague years nearly all the additional burials were in the summer months. The 1579 outbreak saw 30 burials in July, then an incredible 106 in August, and 65 in September, falling off to just fourteen in October. The plague of 1603 saw just eight burials in July: the number rose to 31 in August and peaked in September with 39 burials. In 1666, the burial numbers jumped from eight in June to 49 in July, falling to 36 in August, 26 in September and 23 in October.

The printed figures mean that we can look at the parish of St Helen for the first time, no parish registers of transcripts surviving for this church before 1706. The total population in the 1693 census is given as 338, one of the smallest city parishes. Quite a high proportion of these were presumably inmates of the Great Hospital (the number of whom climbed from 54 in the sixteenth century to 100 in 1742). There were other inhabitants, naturally, including a few families—three baptisms took place in the church between October 1665 and October 1666. The number of burials in the same period was eighteen, just three of whom died from plague. Deaths in the Great Hospital are recorded in the Mayor's Court books (the court would choose who filled the vacancies). There are a number in 1666, but not more than would be expected in a community of the elderly and infirm, and none are said to be from plague: shielding the vulnerable appears to have worked.

Clearly such a heavy mortality would have a dramatic effect on the life of the survivors. Inevitably, there would be many orphans, and also single parent families, so that one might expect much re-marrying. One example is that of the Quaker Thomas Buddery, mentioned earlier. The records show that on 26 May 1667 he remarried, his new bride being Sarah Frost. She was a plague widow herself, having married William Frost at St Peter Mancroft in1650 (her maiden name was Howlett). Later they lived in St Peter Parmentergate and William died there at the height of the plague, being buried on 12 September. The Quaker marriage of Thomas and Susan took place on 26 May 1667 at the house of Anne Whitlock in St Augustine's: Anne herself may well have been the widow of the Joseph Whitlock mentioned earlier. The couple's first child, Caleb Buddery, was born in St Augustine's parish in 1668.

Unions between bereaved spouses were common after plague outbreaks. It is not always possible to quantify this as many parishes, including for example St Benedict, St Julian and St Peter Mancroft, do not specify whether people getting married were single or widowed.

However, most parishes do give marital status, though not always consistently for all couples. At All Saints, the status is given of 26 people getting married in the pre-plague year of 1664: seven were widows or widowers, nineteen were single people. In 1667, after the plague had disappeared, out of 32 people being married, no less than seventeen were widows or widowers, and fifteen single people. In the small parish of St John Maddermarket there were only three marriages in 1664, everyone involved being single. In 1667, there were eight marriages, involving eleven single people and five widows or widowers. Even in parishes where no marital status is given, the increase in the number of marriages can be seen: from four in 1664 to eight in 1667 in St John Sepulchre, for example. One exception was St Michael at Plea where the number of marriages fell from 40 in 1664 to sixteen in 1667. An unusual feature there was that very few of the marriages were of parishioners, almost all being of people from outside the city: perhaps the idea of 'going up the city' to get married seemed a less attractive option after the plague outbreak in Norwich.

In St Stephen's, too, there was an increase in the number of marriages in general and the number of previously married people being remarried in particular, although the position is complicated by the fact that this too was clearly a fashionable church in which to be married, with several couples coming from outside the parish. In 1664, out of the twelve people married, five were widows/widowers, seven single people. In 1667, 30 people were married in the church, twelve being widows or widowers and eighteen single men or women. Some local parishioners getting remarried in 1667 included:

Dorothy Zouch, widow: her first husband, Francis Zouch, petty chapman, had died of plague in August 1666. They had at least one child, Elizabeth, born in January 1666, so Dorothy was a widow with an eighteen-month old daughter when she married Thomas Coale, single man in June 1667.
Margaret Cooke, widow, whose first husband, Richard Cooke, had died of plague in October 1666.
Margery Grime, widow: her husband John Grime was a long-term resident of

St Stephen's, having been baptised in the parish in 1621. He was an oatmeal maker and the couple had at least two children, John, born in 1655 and Judith. Judith died of plague in October 1666, by which time her father was already dead. There is no record of the burial of John junior, so Margery was probably a widow with at least one child to care for when she remarried in 1667, though at twelve he would have been almost old enough for an apprenticeship. Her new husband was also a widower.

There must have been many similar instances in the Norwich of the later 1660s as men and women responded to the life-changing crisis that had been forced upon them by the sudden and traumatic outbreak of plague in 1665-6.

## Should I Stay or Should I Go?

Wealthy people often had a choice whether to remain in a plague-affected city or to retreat to a country estate: the poor, of course, had no such luxury. We have seen how the Paston family in the fifteenth century discussed in their letters whether to visit a place where there was an outbreak of plague, and wealthy families must have faced the same problem.

Blomefield's description of the 1579 plague gives the impression of aldermen bravely remaining at their posts, even dying in the process. Unfortunately, this is a false picture—no aldermen is known to have died of the plague in 1579. Enough aldermen did remain for city government to function, but this was by no means all of them. Paul Slack estimates that the number of aldermen attending the court in normal times might be about fourteen, but that this could fall to about seven in times of plague. The others were presumably self-isolating in their houses—or had left for the country.[6]

The problems this could cause can be seen in surviving letters relating to the 1665-6 outbreak. Thomas Corie, the Town Clerk, wrote in July 1666: 'we are in a very sad condition and the worse in respect that many of our Aldermen have left us'. He thought the Privy Council should order them to stay at their posts! Not every alderman fled. The burial register for St Andrew's records the burial of Alderman Thomas Norris on 19 October 1665 and of Alderman Francis Norris on 25 August 1666. The latter was in the month when the plague was at its height, so he may have been a victim, but this register does not distinguish plague burials from others. At any rate, he clearly had not fled the city! Sixty years earlier, during the plague year of 1603, another alderman had died 'in post': Robert Rooke was buried in St Stephen's on 10 October, but again we do not know if he died from plague.

Another Norwich letter writer, Robert Scrivener, wrote in July 1665: 'our city looks sadly, most of our chiefest shopkeepers in the market are gone and their shops shut up. I do believe before 10 days come a 4 part of the city will be gone'. Later in the month, Corie reported: 'the plague increaseth daily: and our poor tumultuous, the men of best estates gone'. He estimated that within three weeks at least 3,000 people in the city would be out of work. Nor could they find work in the countryside: people would not employ them for fear that they would bring the plague with them. It was feared that the poor might take violent action: Scrivener thought they might take over empty properties as they were saying 'they will live in better houses than now they do'. There was of course no system of furloughing or unemployment pay, so as unemployment rose, many would become desperate. They had to be helped through rates on the wealthier inhabitants of Norwich, and eventually the city had to borrow money to pay its expenses: as Williamson noted, 'the poor in this place are in better order than formerly but it is money that keeps them so, and as soon as that fails we feare they will be unruly'. He put the situation bluntly: 'We are in greater fear of the poor than the plague'. Fortunately, there was an excellent herring catch at Yarmouth that year, Corie writing '12 herrings a penny here fills many a hungry belly'.

Not all city governors behaved so well. In Exeter, during the plague year of 1625, the newly-elected Mayor refused to serve, fleeing the city together with other officials and wealthy citizens: he and the city's overseer of the poor had to be hauled back by order of the Privy Council. No such dereliction of duty appears to have occurred in Norwich: the Mayor remained at his post supported by sufficient aldermen to carry on city government.

## Plague in the Suburbs

**Heigham** was the most populous suburb in Tudor and Stuart Norwich, especially in the latter part of the period. There were an average of five deaths a year in the first years of the 1570s, with a sudden rise to 28 in 1579, dropping to three in 1580 and two in 1581. It seems clear that this outbreak of plague had reached beyond the city walls. By the early 1630s there were about fifteen burials a year: these included between two and six a year from the 'poor-houses' of Saint Giles and Saint Benets, the old lazar houses outside the walls, so that the average of those native to the parish was about a dozen. The peak year was 1631 with 23, including three from St Benets poor-house, so there was no obvious indication of plague: in 1632 there were only 13 burials, including four from the poor-houses. In the first half of the 1660s, the average number of burials in Heigham was between fourteen and fifteen: in the plague years of 1666 and 1667, the number of burials rose to 23 and nineteen respectively, suggesting that this outbreak did not have a drastic effect in the parish.

The other suburbs had an extremely small population, as the numbers of burials indicate. In **Eaton,** for example, there were six burials in 1577 and none at all in 1578. There were seven burials in the plague year of 1579, not enough to say of itself whether plague had reached it. However, of the seven deaths, no less than five came from one family, the Blyths, and all of these were between 2 May and 16 July, so it looks as if plague had entered into this one Eaton family—and with devastating effects.

The five entries are:

| | |
|---|---|
| 2 May | John Blyth |
| 16 May | Edward Blyth |
| 17 May | Johanna Blyth |
| 23 May | Martha Blyth |
| 16 July | Elizabeth Blyth. |

No relationships are given in the burial entries. However, according to the Eaton parish register, Thomas Blyth married Elizabeth Richardson in Eaton church on 30 January 1569. They had two children baptised there, John in 1574 and Martha in 1578. Edward and Johanna are probably also children, perhaps baptised elsewhere. If so, four children, none more than ten years old, died within three weeks of each other, with their mother following seven weeks later. Thomas Blyth himself appears to have survived.

There were four burials in 1580 in Eaton and just two in 1581. By the 1630s there were rather more burials, between five and six a year in the first half of the decade, peaking at twelve in 1630 and eight in 1634. The plague of the 1660s had no effect on Eaton, just one burial a year in 1664, 1665 and 1666, three in 1667 and none in 1668.

In **Lakenham** too there were just one or two burials a year in the 1660s. There was a slight rise in 1666, perhaps suggesting a few plague deaths: although none is so described. The burials mainly occurred in the last third of the year: two in July, two in September and two in November. However, each of the six has a different surname so there was no parallel here to the Blyth family's tragedy.

**Cringleford** was also extremely small. There were no burials at all between 1570 and 1578. There were just three in 1579, two in one month—John Ponnell on 17 March and William Boston on 27 March. Boston's son [unnamed] was buried on 27 July. Burials then returned to their normal rate, one in 1580, one in 1581 and then none at all until 1587. The 1665 plague also had little effect in Cringleford. The burial entries for 1665 do include 'John Allen a stranger dyed in the highway supposed of the plague the 20th August and was buried 21st August 1665'; stranger is probably used here in its more usual sense of 'someone from outside' rather than specifically referring to the Dutch and Walloon immigrants. If it was feared the contagion would spread from this corpse, this was soon allayed: there were no other burials in Cringleford in the last 10 days of August, nor in the following three months. Burial registers do not survive for the period for Thorpe, Trowse, Sprowston, Catton and Taverham. The burial register for Earlham contains no entries for the 1660s.

## Funerals and Plague Pits

Funerals of plague victims were generally conducted at night or early in the morning: this was both to avoid the danger of infection as the bearers carried the body through the streets and also to restrict the number of mourners: as the immediate relatives of the dead person would have been quarantined within the family house, they could not, in any case, have attended. In his well-known diary, Samuel Pepys wrote of his fear of meeting corpses being carried through London streets at night—but also of occasionally seeing such dismal processions in the daytime, so the rules cannot always have been strictly observed. The Privy Council Orders of 1666 prohibited public gatherings such as funerals.

The 1666 Orders also said that bodies were only to be buried in large churchyards, where there was space for a special area to be assigned to plague victims, away from other burials. Plague victims were not to be buried in churches themselves, nor in small churchyards. Many burials in London took place in specially constructed pits. These are described in Daniel Defoe's book 'A Journal of the Plague Year', and some remain as open spaces to this day. I have seen no reference to any plague pits in Norwich in any document. As we have seen, many thousands of plague victims are listed in the Norwich burial registers of the Norwich parish churches in the sixteenth and seventeenth centuries. The natural assumption is that these people were buried in the churchyard of the parish in which their burials were registered.

One possible plague pit was discovered at Lakenham in 1796, where about a hundred skeletons—skulls and other bones—were found when labourers were digging in a field belonging to James Crowe[7]. Among the skeletons was found a trade token of Charles Reeve, a Norwich shoemaker, which had the date 1664. This would suggest that the burials might be of victims of the 1666 plague, the token being dropped by one of the bearers as he carried out his grim work. Faden's map of 1797 shows the Crowe family property as being in the Hall Road area of Lakenham.

As a further complication, the *Norfolk Heritage Explorer* website does not mention a find in Lakenham, but refers to the discovery at the end of the eighteenth century of a group of about a hundred burials further out from the centre of Norwich, in Keswick, near the Harford Toll gate just beyond Harford Bridge (close to the present superstore). It speculates that this might be a plague pit but does not mention a trade token and gives no indication of the possible date: indeed, the Keswick part of the site suggests the pit was medieval. Are these two separate possible pits, or garbled versions of the same discovery? It could be significant that Keswick lies just outside the liberty of the city of Norwich, which ended at Harford Bridge, although, as Faden's map shows, there were very few inhabitants living so far from the walled city even 150 years after the last outbreak of plague. The descriptions of the two sound very different: the Lakenham find is said to have been found by labourers digging in a field, the Keswick skeletons to have been discovered during the demolition of a public house: however, it seems very unlikely there would have been *two* discoveries of such a large number of skeletons made within a few years of each other.

As a pure speculation, I wonder if these were the bodies of some of the 217 people recorded as having died in the pest-house in 1666. I have quoted a Mayor's Court decision in the 1630s that those who died in the pest-house were to be buried at St Peter Southgate. However, the burial registers of that church do not mention any burials from the pest-house and the 1666 victims are certainly not recorded there: the register simply does not include anywhere near enough names. Were they buried in the churchyard unrecorded, or does the Lakenham/ Keswick find represent a plague pit outside the walls of the city?

While on the subject of plague pits, some people think the name of the open space in front of the Cathedral—Tombland—has arisen because plague victims (usually of unspecified date) were buried there: the child Leo Colston in L.P. Hartley's novel 'The Go-Between', who was fascinated by the name, presumably thought that this was the case. Unfortunately, this is simply not true: the word Tombland has nothing to do with tombs. It derives from a Scandinavian word meaning 'empty space' and was given to the area long before the plague arrived in Norwich.

## Medical Services

The greatest difference between 'then' and 'now' lies in healthcare. There was of course no National Health Service and very few doctors, who were expensive—most ordinary people would live and die without seeing one. All you could do if you caught the plague was to go to bed and hope to recover. This means that just about everybody who died did so at home. The 1579 Privy Council Orders were printed and issued with accompanying medical advice. This was a mixture of common sense and a recommendation of herbs to be taken either as prevention or as a cure: there were, naturally, no drugs that could be taken. The advice included:

> Cleanse the air inside infected houses with combinations of herbs like dried rosemary, juniper, bay leaves, rue and wormwood. (A concoction of these herbs in vinegar could be held to the nose when walking through the streets.)

Keep clothes clean and aired.

Drink a cordial made with vinegar and cinnamon. (Those too poor to buy the herbs were advised to eat bread and butter—the butter was thought to be a preservative against plague.)

If plague sores do develop, rub them with scabious, or with a mixture made from mallow leaves and camomile flowers.

There were no hospitals as we know them. Institutions with the name 'hospital'—like the Great Hospital in Bishopgate and Norman's Hospital in St Paul's parish—were much more like modern care homes, places for the elderly and infirm to see out their last days. As we have seen records, show that shielding the vulnerable was certainly practised at the Great Hospital.

The few medical professionals in the city did risk their lives in caring for the sick. Some physicians and their families died of the plague. The physician who died in St Stephen's parish was John Corbett, buried 19 September 1666. In St Gregory's, Henry Bokenham, Doctor of Physic, lost a wife and two children in 1666 a daughter Elizabeth being buried on 16 September, a son Reginald on 3 October, and his wife Elizabeth on 2 November, all from plague. The doctor himself survived, as did his infant son Thomas, who had been baptised on 20 January 1666.

In the absence of a comprehensive medical service, some people panicked and turned to superstitious cures. Daniel Defoe in his 'Journal of a Plague Year' mocked those citizens of London who had the magic word ABRACADABRA put on their houses to ward off the plague in 1665: the fact that they did so suggests desperate people turning to the only possible remedy that they thought might help them. At a more local level, a 'wizard' living in the plague-ridden parish of St Peter Parmentergate came before the Mayor's Court in Norwich in 1666. His name was John Booth, and he was accused of being a wizard by the Mayor's Court on 24 March. He had extracted 2s. 6d. from a Hugh Skoyles presumably a dissatisfied customer, who brought the complaint against him: however, it is not said if the 'cure' was connected with plague. Skoyles died of the plague in the summer of 1666 so that any fears he had were well founded.

## The Privy Council Orders of 1666

New 'Orders' for the prevention of the plague were issued by the Privy Council in 1666, the first full set of Orders since 1579. They included some extremely harsh measures: the Privy Council was determined to do everything possible to establish control over the epidemic. I have modernised the spelling.

RULES AND ORDERS to be observed by all Justices of Peace, Mayors, Bayliffs, and other Officers for prevention of the spreading of the Infection of the PLAGUE.

Published by His Majesties Special Command.

[Orders 1-5 say that no stranger could enter a town unless they had a certificate of health. No furniture was to be removed from an infected house. There were to be no public gatherings such as funerals and all houses were to be kept clean.]

6.  That Fires in moveable Pans, or otherwise, be made in all necessary public Meetings in Churches, &c. and convenient Fumes to correct the Air be burnt thereon.

7.  That care be taken that no unwholesome Meats, stinking Fish, Flesh, musty Corn, or any other unwholesome Food be exposed to sale in any Shops or Markets.

8.  That no Swine, Dogs, Cats or tame Pigeons be permitted to pass up and down in Streets, or from house to house, in places Infected.

9.  That the Laws against Inn-Mates be forthwith put in strict execution, and that no more Alehouses be Licensed then are absolutely necessary in each City or place, especially during the continuance of this present Contagion.

10. That each City and Town forthwith provide some convenient place remote from the same, where a pest-house, huts, or sheds may be erected, to be in readiness in case any Infection should break out; which if it shall happen to do, That able and faithful Searchers and Examiners be forthwith provided and Sworn to Search all suspected bodies, for the usual signs of the plague, viz. Swellings or Risings under the Ears or Arm-pits, or upon the groins; Blains, Carbuncles, or little Spots, either on the Breast or back, commonly called Tokens.

11. That if any House be Infected, the sick person or persons be forthwith removed to the said pest-house, sheds, or huts, for the preservation of the rest of the Family: And that such house (though none be dead therein) be shut up for forty days, and have a Red Cross, and Lord have mercy upon us, in Capital Letters affixed on the door, and Warders appointed, as well to find them necessaries, as to keep them from conversing with the sound.

12. That at the opening of each Infected house (after the expiration of the said Forty Days) a White Cross be affixed on the said door, there to remain

Twenty days more; during which time, or at least before any stranger be suffered to lodge therein, That the said house be well Fumed, Washed and Whited all over within with Lime; And that no Clothes, or Household stuff be removed out of the said house into any other house, for at least Three months after, unless the persons so Infected have occasion to change their habitation.

13. That none dying of the Plague be buried in Churches, or Church-yards (unless they be large, and then to have a place assigned for that use (where other bodies are not usually buried) Boarded or Paled in Ten foot high) but in some other convenient places, and that a good quantity of unslaked Lime be put into the Graves with such bodies, and that such Graves be not after opened within the space of a year or more, less they infect others.

14. That in case any City, Borough, Town or Village be so visited and Infected, that it is not able to maintain its own poor, That then a Rate be forthwith made by the adjoining Justices of the Peace, and confirmed at the very next Quarter Sessions, for that use, upon the neighbouring Parishes, according to the Statute 1 James, so that such visited poor may have sufficient Relief; want and nastiness being great occasions of the Infection.

15. That you your selves use your utmost endeavours, not only to see these Directions punctually observed, and be in a readiness to render an Account as often as you shall be required, but that you strictly enjoyn all high Constables, petty Constables, Headboroughs and other Officers, to execute their respective Duties according to their places; and if any shall fail herein, to use the utmost severity against them according to Law.

What relates to Physicians, surgeons, and such other persons as are necessary for the preservation and help of such who shall be Infected, the same is left to your particular care and direction.

Lastly, That you take special care, that not only the Monthly Fasts, but that the public prayers on Wednesdays and Fridays also, be strictly and constantly observed according to his Majesties Proclamation; And that such Collections as shall be then made, be strictly applied to the relief and necessities of the poor in Infected places, by which means God may be inclined to remove his severe hand both from amongst you and us.

We know that the Norwich aldermen studied these orders: in June 1666, a committee of aldermen was formed for 'ordering the pesthouse' and for putting the Privy Council orders into effect. However, before these draconian rules could be fully applied, the crisis was over. The plague, endemic in England for just over 300 years, never returned.

## Notes

1    NRO, 10f/7.

2    NRO, MC 1/107.

3    *William Hudson and J C Tingey, Records of the City of Norwich, vol II page cv.*

4    Ralph Houlbrooke *Death, Religion and the Family in England 1480-1750* (2000 edition) pp.74, 96. Elizabeth survived, later becoming Lady Elizabeth Delaval: her memoirs have been published by the Surtees Society.

5    NRO, MC 2800/1, dated 29 June 1579 and sent from the relative safety of Blickling.

6    Slack, *op. cit.* p.260.

7    *Norfolk Chronicle* 27 February 1796. Some books and websites cite early nineteenth century sources as their reference for this find, such as the *Norfolk and Norwich Remembrancer* and *Norwich in Miniature*: however, these just repeat the *Norfolk Chronicle* article.

# Conclusion

NO one could have known it at the time, but the outbreak of plague in Norwich in 1665 to 1667 was to be the last. Plague disappeared from England and, eventually from Western Europe: the last major outbreak is often said to be that at Marseilles in 1720.

This seems to have been, at least in part, the result of imposing strict quarantine. In 1667, the *London Gazette* reported on the fighting between Venetians and Turks in Crete: Venetian soldiers were strictly forbidden to take clothing or any other booty from dead Turkish soldiers or to meddle with their bodies. The historian Robin Briggs wrote:

> By the end of the [seventeenth] century western Europe had achieved one striking success, with the virtual elimination of bubonic plague, the great terror of the previous centuries; this seems to have resulted primarily from the introduction of very tight quarantine in the ports and along the land frontier with the Ottoman Empire.[1]

However, as Brian Fagan thought, there were other causes of the disappearance of plague from Western Europe. Writing of an outbreak in southeastern Europe in the early nineteenth century, he comments:

> the plague never affected western Europe, despite the poor harvests and widespread hunger, partly because of strict quarantine measures at eastern frontiers and Mediterranean ports, but also because of critical improvements in domestic hygiene, such as the widespread use of masonry, brick and tile instead of wood, earth and straw in towns and cities.[2]

The plague had first come into Norwich in 1349. It must have had the impact of a nuclear war, with perhaps half the population of the city dying in a few months. It had dramatic effects in the villages around the city, now the suburbs, as well. Later plagues could be almost as devastating, especially that of 1579 when perhaps 40% of the population died. Outbreaks might affect specific parts of the city very badly, while other parts remained almost unaffected. Death rates in a bad year could easily claim a quarter or even a third of the inhabitants of a parish or even the entire city. All the parish churches would have seen tragic scenes, with an almost continual procession of funerals in some, such as St

Julian, St Peter Mancroft, and in St Stephen, where the graveyard is today crossed by thousands of shoppers making their way to Chapelfield shopping centre. In Norwich, the ghosts of the past are all around us.

At first the plague was seen as an Act of God, and the only remedy, apart from prayer, was to run away—if there was anywhere to go. By the later sixteenth century, the city authorities were taking active steps to combat plague: whether because of these, or for some other reason such as climate change, the plague did not return after 1666.

The Guildhall played a key role in the Tudor and Stuart plagues. Every Saturday and Wednesday, the Mayor's Court met and made decisions. The room in which they met still survives, and is a good place to think about the city's past. It is the chamber at the east (lower) end of the first floor, with a chequerwork pattern of flint and freestone on the outside. Inside, many of the fittings are still as they were when the aldermen met to decide how to try to fight the plague in Norwich in Tudor and Stuart times.

The chief weapon used by aldermen trying to fight the plague in Tudor and Stuart Norwich was **isolation**. This was strictly enforced. If a plague death occurred in a house, everyone in the house (family members, apprentices, servants) had to remain within the house until the period of quarantine passed. If another member of the household caught plague, the quarantine period would be extended. There were no exceptions: household members could not leave to take exercise or to go shopping. Windows and doors of a house might be nailed up and a watchman might be placed outside to stop anyone entering or leaving an infected house.

Houses had no refrigeration, of course, and no running water, so isolation was even harder four centuries ago than in the twenty-first century. The city authorities recognised that a household could not be expected to survive on what was in the house. They undertook to provide food and drink to each infected house and, if the household was too poor to pay, the city would do so.

Other measures included applying **lockdown**. The Privy Council never attempted to impose a national lockdown, but individual cities like Norwich could do so whenever local authorities thought it appropriate. It was easy to do because the city was surrounded by the medieval city wall, and all the gates in the wall could be controlled. The concern was not that infected people might leave the city but that people from towns where plague was active might arrive in Norwich bringing the plague with them. To prevent this, people might be banned from entering the city if they came from a town where there was a high rate of infection, or they might be required to produce a certificate that they came from an uninfected house.

**Social distancing** was also practiced. Key workers who were in close contact with the infected had to carry a wand to show that they were high-risk: presumably people could keep well clear if they wished. **Shielding** of the vulnerable also took place, principally the elderly and infirm in the Great Hospital. One of the great differences between Norwich four centuries ago and the city today was that the population was much younger. Few people lived to be old. There were no drugs, no doctors, no care homes—apart from the Great Hospital and the former lazar houses.

Education was quite different four centuries ago and few children would be going to school at all. However, the risks that schools posed were recognised and measures taken. Regulations in the 1630s said that schools 'near any place infected' should be closed. During an outbreak of plague in the city in 1631, schools in Heigham and in West Wymer ward (the St Benedict's Street area) were closed as a precaution, but in the much more severe outbreak of 1666 all schools were closed.

There does not seem to have been a general closure of places of entertainment. If a case of plague involved someone living in a public house, that inn was locked up like any other house where there was infection. Other forms of entertainment, like travelling shows, always had to get a licence from the Mayor's Court—even in good years they were often chary of issuing these, citing the danger of the spread of plague as a reason for refusing a licence: in June and July 1633, for example, three groups of players were paid for *not* playing in the city. In times of plague, they naturally refused to allow such entertainments.

Churches remained open. They were the main vehicle of communicating news as the clergyman could read out announcements and new regulations concerning plague. Of course, there were risks. Thomas Corie noted in October 1666 that the Presbyterians and Independents could 'find no other place for their conventicle the last Sunday but the next house to the plague, so that a wall did but part them.' He says that they were dispersed by Authority but does not say whether it was on health grounds or because of disapproval of their religious views. He noted that there were 120 to 140 people gathered, presumably without social distancing. Such large gatherings must have brought great danger of the spread of the infection.

The Court tried to prevent crowds gathering for funerals, although there was never a fixed limit on those attending. Different rules were set out at different times—sometimes it was forbidden to toll the church bells, sometimes it was ordered that funerals of plague victims had to take place before sunrise or after sunset.

The great French historian Fernand Braudel painted a grim picture of

European cities in time of plague:

> At the first sign of the disease the rich whenever possible took hurried flight to their country houses; no-one thought of anything but himself. The poor remained alone, penned up in the contaminated town where the State fed them, isolated them, blockaded them and kept them under observation.[3]

As far as Norwich goes, this seems exaggerated. A distinction should be drawn between rich county families like the Pastons and the Hobarts, who could live in the town or the country as they pleased, and the city magistrates who had a *duty* to remain and to try and fight the plague. Some of these may have fled, but about half the aldermen continued to attend the court even in the worst plague years. It is true that the plague affected the poor more than the rich, the main reason being that overcrowded conditions made it harder to self-isolate.

'Lock-down', 'social distancing', 'self-isolation'. The words would be strange to the aldermen of Norwich four hundred years ago but the ideas behind them would be familiar as they struggled to control outbreaks of plague in their city. The crises the plague caused, and the effectiveness or otherwise of the measures taken against it, provide us with lessons for any future epidemic that may affect the city. As always, there is a great deal to learn from our past: people who are not willing to learn from history repeat the same mistakes all over again.

**Notes**

1    Robin Briggs, 'Embattled Faiths' in Euan Cameron ed, *Early Modern Europe: an Oxford History* (2001 edition) p.199.

2    Brian Fagan, *The Little Ice Age* (2000) p.178.

3    Fernand Braudel, *The Structures of Everyday Life* (1981 edition) p.85.

# Appendix 1

### New Freemen of Norwich in 1349, from the Old Free Book

### Translation of St Edward:

Henry Bacon
Stephen Patrick de Bokenham
William Broun, ferour
John Corald, hatter
Robert Dade de Repynghal
Nicholas de Herringfleet, tailor
Adam de Linne, skinner
Robert de Metton, coteler
William de Reveshal
Henry de Tivetshall
Francis Spicer
Thomas Mortimer de Bernham
Roger de Bressingham, baxter
Gilbert de Corf, marbrer
John Kippyng
Gilbert de Seckford, mercer
John de Wells, sherman

Geoffrey de Dunham
Thomas Dussing de Kirkeby
John de Elton
Richard Gauge
Thomas Gerard de Thurston
Alan de Gillingham de Gowthorpe
John Neve de Hadelye
Walter de Horstead, clerk
William Loughf de South Creake
Alexander de Molton
John Page
Richard Patrick
Richard de Riston
Bartholomew Suneman
John de Thorpendel
William Ward
John de Wicklewood

Also three names, then crossed through:

John de Marton, skinner
Robert de Pickenham, skinner
John Reynald de Southfield

### Saturday after Circumcision:

William de Acre de Westacre
Henry de Bastwick, webster
Robert Broun
Simon Clerke de Ingoldisthorpe
William de Derham
Richard de Dilham
Geoffrey Dokesson of Cecil de Marlingford
William de Drayton

Hugh Curzoun de Aldeburgh
William Baker
John de Bracondale, mercer
Henry Spynk de Brooke
Walter Broun de East Tuddenham
John de Brundall
William de Cantley, barber
Richard de Deopham, smith
Alexander de Derham
John Latimer de Dilham
William le fuller de Pulham
Thomas Gottes
Walter de Gressenhall
Edward de Yarmouth, saddler
Geoffrey Sewale de Letheringsett
Thomas son of John Nicholas de Wroxham

James Shethere
[Alan Southorp de Gillingham]
William de Sporle
William Swon
John Sylvester, cordwainer
Thomas Tassemaker,
Peter son of Thomas Tassemaker,
John de Ware
Nicholas Wynde
Thomas de Wynkefeld, baxter
Walter Wyth

[William de Acre de Westacre]
Semannus de Beccles
[Robert Broun]
John de Catton, litster
James de Crownesthorp
[Richard de Deopham, smith]
[John Latimer de Dilham]
David Fisshman
Robert de Gunton
Richard Heyward
[Thomas Dussyng de Kirkeby]
Thomas de Leighton Buzzard, coteler
[Geoffrey Sewale de Letheringsett]
Geoffrey Malesel
John de Marton, skinner
William Marwe
[Thomas son of John Nicholas de Wroxham]
Robert de Pickenham, skinner
Henry de Playford, clerk
John Reynald de Southfield
Thomas Soppe
John de Stratford, leatherworker
William Threckeby
William Turpel
Walter Webbe
John Wolbester

(Names in square brackets have been crossed through.)

# Appendix 2

## Weekly burials from the Mayor's Court Books: June 1579 to February 1580

From the last week in October, the numbers of strangers among the dead are noted.

| date | died | of which strangers |
|---|---|---|
| 1579, 27, June | 56 | |
| 4 July | 66 | |
| 11 July | 98 | |
| 18 July | 133 | |
| 25 July | 167 | |
| 1 August | 244 | |
| 8 August | 268 | |
| 15 August | 352 | |
| 22 August | 226 | |
| 29 August | 331 | |
| 5 September | 298 | |
| 12 September | 288 | |
| 19 September | 208 | |
| 26 September | 275 | |
| 3 October | 230 | |
| 10 October | 241 | |
| 17 October | 249 | |
| 24 October | 144 | |
| 31 October | 89 | 62 |
| 7 November | 94 | 69 |
| 14 November | 45 | 31 |
| 21 November | 40 | 22 |
| 28 November | 53 | 41 |
| 5 December | 58 | blank |
| 12 December | 63 | 48 |
| 19 December | 48 | 35 |

| 26 December | 29 | 24 |
|---|---|---|
| 1580, 2 January | 27 | 23 |
| 9 January | 44 | 35 |
| 16 January | 34 | 27 |
| 23 January | 35 | 28 |
| 30 January | 38 | 29 |
| 6 February | 29 | 20 |
| 13 February | 30 | 24 |
| 20 February | 29 | 24 |
| 27 February | 41 | 26 |

# Appendix 3

**Weekly burials from Mayor's Court Books, April 1625 to January 1626**

| date | total burials | of which strangers | of which plague |
|---|---|---|---|
| 1625, 2 April | 15 | 3 | 0 |
| 9 | 7 | 1 | 0 |
| 16 | 25 | 5 | 0 |
| 23 | 14 | 5 | 0 |
| 30 | 23 | 6 | 0 |
| 7 May | 32 | 6 | 0 |
| 14 | 7 | 1 | 0 |
| 21 | 13 | 4 | 0 |
| 28 | 30 | 3 | 0 |
| 4 June | 33 | 8 | 0 |
| 11 | 16 | 4 | 0 |
| 18 | 29 | 10 | 0 |
| 25 | 26 | 4 | 0 |
| 2 July | 42 | 10 | 0 |
| 9 | 38 | 6 | 0 |
| 16 | 38 | 10 | 0 |
| 23 | 24 | 2 | 2 |
| 30 | 26 | 6 | 0 |
| 6 Aug | 53 | 10 | 0 |
| 13 | 41 | 3 | 14 |
| 20 | 77 | 12 | 67 |
| 27 | 76 | 8 | 57 |
| 3 Sept | 72 | 10 | 62 |
| 10 | 90 | 13 | 71 |
| 17 | 95 | 10 | 77 |
| 24 | 96 | 14 | 71 |

| 1 Oct | 67 | 6 | 44 |
|---|---|---|---|
| 8 | 91 | 16 | 73 |
| 15 | 72 | 11 | 62 |
| 22 | 69 | 7 | 41 |
| 29 | 44 | 9 | 32 |
| 5 Nov | 52 | 7 | 37 |
| 12 | 53 | 5 | 31 |
| 19 | 46 | 8 | 34 |
| 26 | 31 | 4 | 16 |
| 3 Dec | 30 | 7 | 19 |
| 10 | 40 | 1 | 20 |
| 17 | 33 | 1 | 10 |
| 24 | 15 | 3 | 6 |
| 31 | 31 | 8 | 15 |
| 7 Jan 1626 | 26 | 4 | 11 |
| 14 | 25 | 3 | 10 |
| 21 | 20 | 0 | 7 |
| 28 | 20 | 2 | 7 |

# Appendix 4

**Burials between 3 October 1665 and 3 October 1666, from** *Norwich Records* **(1736), with population figures, 1693**

| parish | pop 1693 | baptisms | burials | plague | |
|---|---|---|---|---|---|
| Peter Southgate | 470 | 14 | 94 | 73 | + |
| Etheldreda | 243 | 9 | 63 | 48 | + |
| Julian | 563 | 8 | 191 | 176 | + |
| Peter Parmentergate | 1376 | 32 | 367 | 317 | + |
| John Sepulchre | 781 | 27 | 88 | 65 | - |
| Michael at Thorn | 865 | 25 | 233 | 202 | + |
| John Timberhill | 668 | 24 | 72 | 46 | - |
| All Saints | 425 | 22 | 71 | 57 | + |
| Stephen | 1769 | 50 | 185 | 138 | - |
| Peter Mancroft | 1953 | 47 | 153 | 107 | - |
| Giles | 910 | 18 | 74 | 66 | - |
| Benedict | 652 | 12 | 29 | 14 | -- |
| Swithin | 496 | 12 | 39 | 23 | -- |
| Margaret | 664 | 17 | 94 | 77 | + |
| Lawrence | 668 | 23 | 70 | 53 | - |
| Gregory | 772 | 18 | 34 | 13 | -- |
| John Maddermarket | 657 | 13 | 54 | 44 | - |
| Andrew | 935 | 25 | 37 | 12 | -- |
| Michael at Plea | 479 | 8 | 17 | 7 | -- |
| Peter Hungate | 267 | 8 | 16 | 8 | -- |
| George Tombland | 722 | 14 | 25 | 13 | -- |
| Simon and Jude | 362 | 7 | 20 | 13 | -- |
| Martin at Palace | 819 | 27 | 53 | 24 | -- |
| Helen | 338 | 5 | 18 | 3 | -- |
| Michael Coslany | 1026 | 28 | 93 | 67 | - |
| George Colegate | 1151 | 18 | 70 | 42 | -- |

| | | | | | |
|---|---|---|---|---|---|
| Clement | 593 | 12 | 37 | 16 | -- |
| Edmund | 370 | 7 | 18 | 4 | -- |
| Mary Coslany | 949 | 30 | 73 | 47 | - |
| Martin at Oak | 1243 | 43 | 132 | 102 | - |
| Augustine | 850 | 20 | 88 | 61 | - |
| Saviour | 710 | 12 | 21 | 8 | -- |
| Paul | 983 | 33 | 68 | 36 | -- |
| James | 416 | 38 | 75 | 46 | + |
| Heigham | 544 | 12 | 17 | 6 | -- |
| Deaths in pest-house | | - | 217 | 217 | |
| MALES | | 360 | 1372 | - | |
| FEMALES | | 358 | 1423 | - | |
| TOTALS | | 718 | 3012 | 2251 | |
| Pockthorpe | 732 | | | | |
| Lakenham | 221 | | | | |
| Eaton | 153 | | | | |
| Earlham | 50 | | | | |
| Hellesdon | 65 | | | | |
| Thorpe in Norwich | 69 | | | | |
| Trowse, Carrow, Bracondale | 258 | | | | |
| Precinct of the Close | 650 | | | | |

Comparison of plague burials with the population in 1693:
+ more than 10%, - between 5% and 10%, -- less than 5%

# Appendix 5

## Norwich plague figures in 1666 from *London Gazette*

| week ending | all burials | burials from plague | pest-house | other |
|---|---|---|---|---|
| Jun 13 | 28 | 18 | 4 | |
| Jun 20 | 38 | 19 | 4 | |
| Jun 27 | 35 | 22 | 5 | |
| Jul 4 | 52 | 38 | 2 | |
| Jul 11 | 80 | 56 | 7 | |
| Jul 18 | 85 | 65 | 20 | Bracondale 2 |
| Jul 25 | 147 | 130 | 7 | |
| Aug 1 | 145 | 125 | 5 | |
| Aug 8 | 187 | 163 | 6 | Cathedral Close 2 |
| Aug 15 | 196 | 177 | 4 | |
| Aug 22 | 218 | 201 | 1 | |
| Aug 29 | 190 | 180 | 1 | |
| Sep 5 | 162 | 147 | 12 | |
| Sep 12 | 154 | 135 | | |
| Sep 19 | 155 | 140 | | |
| Sep 26 | 150 | 139 | | |
| Oct 3 | 115 | 100 | | |
| Oct 10 | 111 | 103 | | |
| Oct 17 | 317 [sic— probably printing error for 137] | 127 | | |
| Oct 24 | 75 | 68 | | |
| Oct 31 | 67 | 58 | | |
| Nov 7 | 65 | 56 | | |
| Nov 14 | 46 | 31 | | |
| Nov 21 | 41 | 30 | | |

| Nov 28 | 19 | 15 | | |
|--------|-----|---------|-------|--|
| Dec 5  | no  | figures | given | |
| Dec 12 | 36  | 23      | | |
| Dec 19 | 17  | 14      | | |
| Dec 26 | 21  | 11      | | |

# Appendix 6

## Burials in three Norwich suburbs in the 1660s

| date | Cringleford | Lakenham | Heigham |
|------|-------------|----------|---------|
| 1660 | 0 | - | 12 |
| 1661 | 1 | - | 19 |
| 1662 | 2 | - | 22 |
| 1663 | 3 | - | 9 |
| 1664 | 4 | - | 12 |
| 1665 | 5 | - | 16 |
| 1666 | 3 | 7 | 23 |
| 1667 | 0 | 3 | 19 |
| 1668 | 0 | 8 | 15 |
| 1669 | 0 | 8 | 14 |

The burial register for Lakenham only survives from 1666.

# Map B

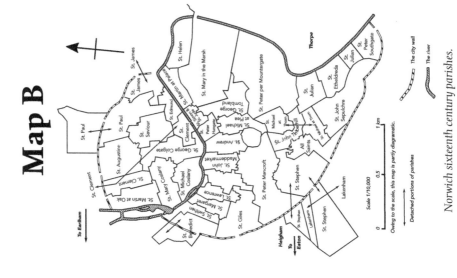

*Norwich sixteenth century parishes.*

# Map A

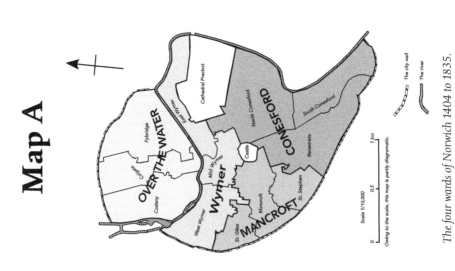

*The four wards of Norwich 1404 to 1835.*

# Index